Westech Media:

PROMOTE YOUR BUSINESS

A Technical Guide To Digital Marketing

Ofer Oved

Published by
L.R. Price Publications Ltd.
27 Old Gloucester Street,
London, WC1N 3AX
www.lrpricepublications.com

ISBN: 9781916467972

Westech Media

Westech Media is a UK digital marketing agency in the UK that specialises in promoting small and local businesses.

Over the last ten years it has helped hundreds of clients to grow their businesses, increase their sales and gain more customers.

If you are a small business owner and would like assistance promoting your business then contact Westech Media today.

Website: www.westech.media

UK Head Office: 0203 0519505

Email: email@westech.media

"Dedicated to our clients."

Westech Media:

Promote Your Business

A Technical Guide To Digital Marketing

Introduction

The world is changing.

Digital technologies and platforms have become significant influences in our lives, affecting our behavior as well as our social, professional and cultural environment, our as well as our personal development and consumption.

Business must also adapt to these changes. Luckily there is still time, as the changes are gradual with an uneven change across the entire activity of the global population as a whole.

However, these changes will have a tipping point, a point in time from which the market looks and behaves differently.

Once this tipping point is reached, there is no going back. Businesses that have failed to adapt will die and other business will take their place.

The tipping point for businesses will occur within the next five years.

This book will provide a technical guide to digital marketing covering: Online advertising, Content marketing, Social marketing, Mobile marketing and E-commerce.

Contents

Chapter One

Digital Marketing

Strategic Insights & Trends

Building Blocks of the New Marketing World

The new structure of the marketing field stands on the following cornerstones which are different from those we have known and were used to for years. This chapter briefly describes the anchors / terms that should be taken into account when considering marketing moves in the new era.

Relations

In the digital age where the consumer has more alternatives and less time, the method of one-way communication has suffered a lethal blow. The brand's singularly aimed shout to get the consumer's attention is no longer effective. A brand has to be committed to creating a relationship with its target audience. A relationship based on familiarity, value and listening. Without these, effective marketing activity cannot exist.

Conversions

In order to establish relationships, brands need to establish a permanent digital presence that will serve as its "meeting point" with its customers – a website, a mobile application, a brand blog, social networking arena, a YouTube brand channel, and so on. A means of meeting and creating the necessary relationship with potential customers. From the moment that meeting point is in place, dealing with customers' needs involves the four following stages:

- Conversion A – **from people to visitors**. At this stage, the brand wishes to bring as many people as possible to visit its digital assets.
- Conversion B – **from visitors to users**. The task at this step is to convince visitors to get involved in your assets. This can be done through signing up for the site, joining the brand on Facebook, or joining its community on Instagram or Twitter. This marks the first sign of a potential relationship.
- Conversion C – **from friends / users to customers**. This step looks to change users to customers. In other words, take out your wallet...
- Conversion D – at this stage we go the extra mile and try to convince our

friends or customers to become brand promoters. Promoters who will help us distribute our content, talk about our product and convince their friends to follow suit.

Digital marketing is largely based on these four conversion stages, with each stage based on a detailed and quantified work plan. In other words: it's all about conversions.

Permission

In the digital age, the consumers have the power. When it comes to content, shopping, community services, etc., they have a multitude of options. They find a way to ignore marketing messages that threaten to overwhelm them. We are approaching a point where any marketing initiative will potentially be subject to permission alone. If a brand fails to receive permission to market – its message will not be accepted.

The good news is that brands have many points of permission – convincing the consumer to download their app or sign up for their website, follow the brand on social network, or sign up for its blog – will be considered permission. At this point, the brand becomes "marketing authorized" with reasonable listening potential.

Value

As part of the need to establish a relationship with consumers, brands have to provide customers with a real, customized value. One that will be relevant to the target audience and convince it to be involved. In the digital age, the dialog between brand and consumer cannot be based solely on the product you are trying to sell. There has to be an added value – usually expressed in the content world that the brand provides its customers.

Simultaneous Usage

The digital natives – those who were born from the 1980s onward into the digital age – have adopted the use of multiple devices and platforms simultaneously. They skip from using their computer to their smartphone and from there to their tablet. They jump from talking on WhatsApp to virtual meetings on Facebook, Instagram, Snapchat and music and the like. It is difficult to catch them in one place and therefore brands need to create a constant presence on all devices and platforms.

Micro-clusters/activities/budgets

Smart brands no longer speak in terms of broad reach and frequency of exposure as was the practice in the time of traditional marketing. The up-to-date way to create a market dialog is to define a micro-segment – a focused, characterized human cluster, and reach it through micro-publishers – small and characteristic media – such as bloggers or YouTubers who will not bring your advertising message to millions but will link your brand to a small and attentive audience, all with a relatively small and controlled budget. In other words, the efficient formula abandons the mass media that target millions and instead directs the budget to moves that define micro-segments and uses micro-publishers. A long tail of small, efficient and measurable activities.

Gatekeepers / Influencers

Reaching your target audience entails listening. Traditional media do not guarantee listening. People who influence people, readers loyal to their blogger, followers influenced by unofficial leaders – all have turned the media field into a long line of small players that will bring your message to the desired audience.

FOC / Tribes

A friend who recommends a product influences us much more than any advertisement, even if he is not a close friend. We are all influenced by networks of unknown people on social media. A brand that succeeds in penetrating these circles of social influence and / or groups opens its door to members of the tribe and enjoys an organic distribution of its marketing message – assuming it carries value for its members.

Emotional Marketing

Terms such as: Engagement marketing /Experiential marketing /Event marketing /On-ground marketing – are becoming a very important element in brands' marketing activities.

This is a marketing and advertising campaign aimed at clearly defined audiences which is supposed to help the brand create a range of emotions among potential customers that will support goals such as remembering, sympathy, prominence, developing a relationship between the brand and its customers, who're leaning towards buying.

The Passionate Segment

The next few years will see most marketers abandoning some of their target audiences in favor of marketing for one – **the passionate segment** – those who crave the category, those who try its products, read every article published on it, talk about other related products and distribute the content they receive from the category brands. These are the best, most loyal customers – and most importantly it is up to you to turn them into your brand promoters. Focusing on this one segment will earn you the best ROMI – Return on Marketing Investment, serving as the basis for all your digital marketing activities. Social Marketing activity will help you locate and mark these important people.

Social Proof of Quality – SPOQ

A super term that describes all channels in which people influence others in their purchasing decisions and preference of a product or service. In the digital age, "social density" – positively, of course – is worth more than any advertising campaign. It serves as a quality signal. Research shows that 77% of people read users' feedback before making their shopping decision. Now it's time for brands to join in and include it in their marketing plan.

Generation Y/Z

The Millennial generation – the first generation born to digital – is the most important one for brand and media companies. Both this and the previous generation create a different, elusive consumer profile – with less television watching, limited loyalty to brands, they demand sharing of products and content, impatient and less tolerant of unpleasant buying experiences, and require both transparency and involvement.

Both young generations – Y and Z – are similar in the hurdles they create for brands and media companies, yet there are significant differences between them.

Overlapping / Native Advertising

Two types of advertising formats have been dominant (and still are) throughout the years: the first one is **Break** (advertising before and after content, i.e., on TV) and the second one is **Nearby** (advertisement next to content – i.e. in the press). These two formats are about to disappear from our lives. They are no longer effective. Digital native users have long ago found the way to ignore these formats which are about to be replaced by **"overlapping"** – a format where content and brand come together to provide value to the user. This format is usually expressed in content produced by the brand, focusing on providing branded value to a defined micro-segmented audience.

Shakable Ads

Studies show that the generations Y and Z have no time for ads. The only way to win a reasonable chance of gaining their attention is to produce short ads of maximum five seconds long. It is not easy to convey a message in such tight constraints, but it is possible. More importantly – it is necessary. By the way, if you are looking for a unique start-up idea, you could set up a creative agency (with technological capabilities) that specializes in producing video ads of up to five seconds.

The Age of Discovery

Looking at the evolution of the media in recent decades, it all began with us learning almost everything through it. We got to know about new fashions, business opportunities, the state of the economy, news, sports, gossip, and so forth from the traditional media. Then came Google, which told us not to wait for the media to find out about it but use its search engine to do the work for us – that was the age of searching. Then came social networks that brought with them social discovery – which enables us to collect information and content while hanging out in social networks. We learn about the world from our social friends and their friends' friends. So, if a brand is looking to be relevant and to control some information, it should be highly active in the social networks. Don't advertise there. Live there.

DDP – Detachable Digital Publishers

Traditional media companies such as CNN, for example, know that the young audiences no longer visit their home websites. To reach the digital audience, these companies need to bring their content to the users instead of bringing the users to their content.

How do you do it?

Publishers should be “freaks” – break up pieces of content, pack them up very small and channel them to young people, spreading these channels on relevant platforms. These can include platforms such as Snapchat or any other where you can meet young people and also implement a relevant business model.

MESSAGE VISUALIZATION

The young generations lead a communication model based on visuals – images, animations and mainly video clips. These constitute the main formats that lead the discourse, sharing and distribution. Brands should take that into account when designing their work plans.

AR

Augmented reality technology (much more so than virtual reality) has become a significant tool for marketers and brands:

Promoting business on the street, integrating game elements to connect a brand with consumers, adding elements that enable a remote experience of the product, expanding information about a product at a sale point, etc.

– all render the old technology meaningless in the work plans of businesses and brands.

The Age of Voice

Voice search, voice-based interaction between consumer and brand and other voice-based services are now becoming the industry's leading user interface format. Here, too, brands need to be ready and targeted on upgrading their relationship with customers and consumers.

Pronsumers

The digital age has made us all into two-headed creatures – we are simultaneously producers and consumers of content at the same time. We consume content but at the same time know and want to contribute content and influence our friends on the net. Brands should allow us to contribute content on their assets. This is a basic condition in building relations between brands and potential customers.

Chat Bot

A Chat Bot is actually a computer program that performs a defined task automatically. Bots can collect information for you from various sources, can answer questions, advise you, and of course help you in an efficient and fast online shopping process. This effective format could substitute or add to the mobile application activity of brands which are already active. Leading brands claim that it is easy for them to produce bots and ride on existing platforms of social networks such as Facebook or messaging platforms like Viber. The development, as well as the marketing processes, is simpler.

Blockchain / Crypto

The next revolution will be based on a technological player who will create a new tool to form relationships in the digital world – **Cryptocurrency.** This is currency created with technological means whose value is not determined by that of a commodity or a central body but rather by agreement within a network of users (Bitcoin, Ripple, etc.).
This technology opens a significant playground for media companies and advertisers to initiate a reward-based dialog with consumers. Media companies will be able to reward content producers as well as loyal readers, and brands will be able to reward those who followed their advertisement to the end – all with currencies in an utmost reliable and secure system.

Programmatic/Automatic

Content creation, campaign management, brand social activity management – all are automated. This reduces costs, increases control and analytical possibilities, and above all allows brands to bring all their systems together for absolute budget management and especially data. This trend will make some Eco System players irrelevant.

Visual Search

The next generation of search engines is based on visualization of information. Information is based on the visual study of objects and currently visual search is led by Google. The use is friendly and simple – you turn your camera to the object you are after online or in your actual surrounding and get the relevant information.

The End of Creativity

Targeting and reaching micro-audiences questions the place of creativity, which for many years has been the central backbone of the life of the traditional advertising agency. If a brand is capable of accurately reaching a potential customer while perfectly understanding his needs, desires and consumer profile, there is apparently no need for all that hoo-ha. The targeted offer will do a better job.

"And what about brand image creativity?" some will ask. Following super brands of the digital age will prove that they have positioned themselves by providing value rather than through traditional creativity. Does anyone remember the fancy slogan of Facebook or Google?

Fast Brands

Forget about fast food. Think instead about fast brands. They are the ones which will lead the market. Fast brands should work quickly in all fields:

Quick intelligence creation

Quick creation of a relationship with consumers (who should understand their benefit and value)

Fast / Quick navigation options within brands' digital assets / digital stores

Fast purchase (zero or one click purchasing)

Quick delivery

Quick response (customer relations)

Fast circulation within the community (converting Customers to Promoters)

Creative and marketing people now need to have a new set of skills. Skills that are expressed in their technological understanding, or, in other words – how lightweight and accessible technologies can be used to properly package a brand.

The End of Spray & Pray

Creation and dispersion, or in other words, creativity and spraying here and there, with no definite focus and value, has come to an end. Whatever is not targeted, quantified, relevant, or cannot bring value to a distinct and clear audience, is being replaced by a clear-cut activity based on providing value and maintaining a relationship between brands and customers.

These are the terms and insights that will lead digital marketing in the next few years, most of which I will expand on later in the book.

Chapter Two

Go to Market Plan Structure

Before launching your activity, you should build a strategic digital marketing plan to include several basic components.

First and foremost, brands have no choice but to create a spider strategy to indicate their digital presence – digital assets – through which the brand has a chance to meet its target audience and begin its relationship with potential customers. That is why brands invest a lot of resources and energy in building websites, apps, branded social sites, blogs, and so on. This phase is based on three layers.

Owned Media

During its setting up stage the brand establishes its own media, a virtual meeting place with its audience.

Paid Media

The next stage requires generating traffic to the digital assets through initiated campaigns. Now that there are enough people who have popped in, we would very much like those visitors to have their friends share their experience; this stage is called:

Earned Media

The most typical goal of digital marketing moves lies in the hope to turn our users into promoters, namely supporters of our digital assets, by directing their friends to our site, our apps or our blog and to our brand on social media.

Digital marketing is based on four types of conversions:

From People to Visitors

Creating initial traffic of users to our digital assets. At this stage, no deep involvement or familiarity is happening with our audience. We should therefore dedicate our efforts to promotion and advertising including search engine optimization, programmatic advertising on the web, content-based marketing, mobile advertising and electronic public relations.

From Visitors to Friends or Users

At this point, we would like to start getting to know our visitors and try to initiate a relationship with them. Enticing them to become our friends on Facebook, our followers on Instagram or Twitter or even just register to our website or blog, will be the first step in a relationship on which a market dialog can be established. This stage requires considerable investment in content that engenders involvement and interest, content that stimulates the user to consume our content, and believe that our digital property (website, app, blog, etc.) is an important source of content for him, and therefore he should connect to our assets on a more permanent basis.

From Friends to Customers

After we turned visitors into friends, we want to try and add another layer to this relationship, that of a business dialog. In other words, turn those friends into customers who might spend money and generate new revenues on our assets. We can do that by conversion – products such as coupons, loyalty benefits or digital coins that the consumer can accumulate on his visits to our site, and which can be used in our brand store. For example, a product that moves users from a venue where there is no business dialog to one where there is a chance to do business (a physical or digital store).

From Customers to Promoters

There is no question that the most important and influential message in the digital age comes from our friends or social environment. Our friends, or friends of friends on more distant circles, influence our perceptions and decisions far more than any advertising campaign. In addition, one has to bear in mind that the digital consumer craves sharing and influence. People would like to be involved, share and make a change.

This stage in the Go-to-Market program focuses on decisions and activities aimed at influencing friends / followers / users / customers to help us spread our message and content. In short, distribute, share and become our promoters / brand supporters.

In order to help them help us, we should focus on creating user-friendly UI and UX frames (big sharing buttons, connectivity to all networks, etc.) and create content that stimulates sharing and distribution. For example, video content inspires sharing more than text, short content is distributed more than long content, humor earns more sharing than any other type of content, and content with game elements is often shared more (gamification format).

In fact, this is the whole story of real and effective digital marketing.

Attract-Engage-Convert-Inspire

The correct way to build a long-term digital marketing plan is to produce specific content and methodology for each stage of the conversion sequence.

A set of advertising / promotion activities for the visitors' stage.

A set of attractions and triggers for those who have already visited (for them to become friends / followers / users / promoters)

A set of conversions – moving engines, moving users from a lack of business-related relationship to one which entices the customer to spend money with us.

A set of triggers that will convince customers to become our brand / business promoters.

This the ultimate Go-To-Market plan of the Digital age

How to implement the go-to-market program?

The observation stage:

1. **Start with the first conversion phase observation** – from people to visitors – examine the brand's site, mobile app and social activity performance.

<u>Site Performance:</u>
At this point, we'll examine the site's performance compared to our competitors. You can use tools such as SimilarWeb or Alexa to understand numbers such as visits, time on site and bounce rate. At this point, we'll also

look at organic search performance – we'll select five relevant terms and search for them on a search engine. If your brand does not appear on the first results search page, you should work on your organic search plan.

Mobile Performance:
In the observation stage we will examine our app performance compared to our competitors' performance – use, users' profiles, bounce rate, territories, users' feedback and so on. We will use Google Play data as well as tools such as https://www.appannie.com

We'll also test organic search performance in the app stores – select five relevant terms and search them on the store's search engine. If your brand does not appear on the top three shelves in the store, you need to create a smarter mobile organic search plan.

Social network activity performance:
We will examine brands' performance on social networks compared to our competitors – number of members, followers, comments, engagement sharing performance, etc.

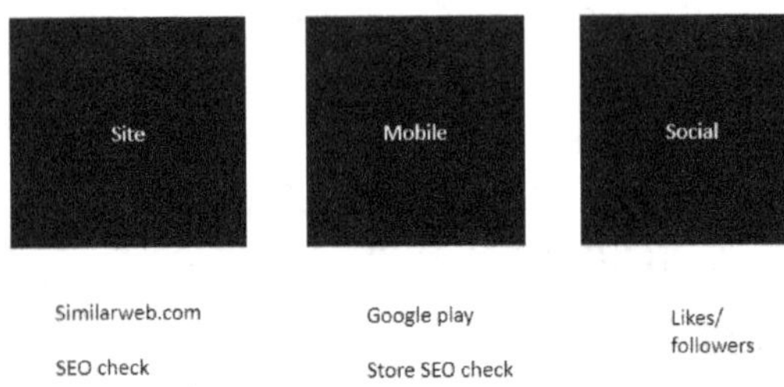

2. Second Conversion Performance Observation – How well do we succeed in converting visitors to friends / followers / users?

Go through all the digital assets of the brand and its competitors – website, mobile, social, blog, etc. – in order to examine the extent to which content and activities are generating sharing and trigger continued use. This is the first step in building a relationship with the target audience.

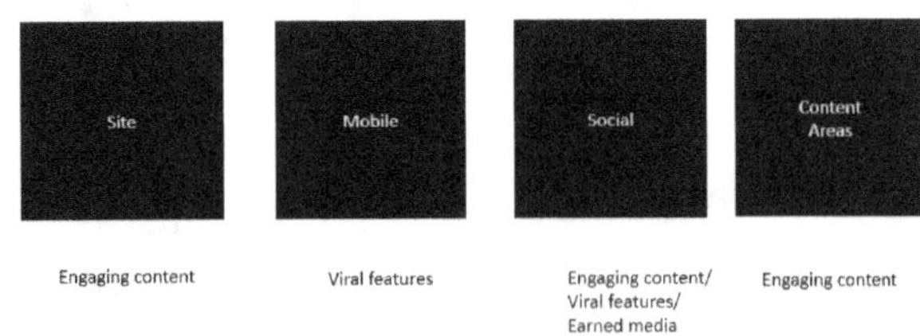

1. **Observing conversion performance from users to customers**
   The next step in the comparative observation task is to examine how well we are doing in moving users to spend money with us and initiate a business-oriented dialog – third conversion – from friends or users to customer status. To what extent does the brand and its competitors use moving tools, such as coupons, special sales offers and the like.
2. **Observation transition performance from customers to brand promoters**
   In the final observation step we examine the extent to which the brand – compared to its competitors – generates a trigger for sharing, feedback of user experiences. In other words, to what extent accurate actions have been taken to convince users to become brand promoters.

<u>The planning stage of the marketing activity based on the findings of these observations:</u>

Conversion A

Based on the performance of this step, we will suggest detailed ways to move more traffic to our digital assets. We will use all means to initiate this traffic – programmatic advertising, social networking, collaboration with influencers, mobile promotion, content-based marketing, organic promotion and search engine optimization, public relations on the web and brand guerrilla activities.

Conversion B & D

In order to turn visitors into users / friends / followers and later persuade them to become brand promoters, it is necessary first to produce engaging and retention-enhancing content and reuse. This means content that produces value to the target audience we have defined for ourselves. The more visual the content the better – video and images – which is the content type that generates more significant distribution and sharing potential. Beyond that, managing the digital assets of the brand should be handled in every respect as a business, including a logical organizational structure consisting of analytics and community content professionals.

Conversion C

At this stage, we will add triggers that will bring users closer to a business dialog with the brand, such as:

Incentive activities – content attractions that may move visitors to our digital properties and bring them closer to purchasing points.

Social shopping – assumes that users are influenced by their network friends (not necessarily close ones) and, in turn, influence others. A brand that knows how to create a long-term relationship with users can be there and impact the users' dialog.

Group purchasing – A brand can invite community members to win a valuable and attractive prize when they initiate the gathering of a large group of buyers in a predefined time range for group campaign. Distribution and response are then almost guaranteed. This is more effective than most campaigns, which use open media.

MPOP – Mobile Proof of Presence, known also as mobile activity check-in. A brand invites users to prove their presence at a branch or store and win a prize (as individuals or as a group). This is an effective tool of moving to a location where they can do business (the brand store or the relevant shelf) when the brand and the user do not have a business relationship (Facebook, for example).

Social Influencers – Influencers are increasingly beginning to serve as an excellent moving tool for brands. Their followers listen to them and a buying recommendation based on listening may work to their advantage.

Chapter Three

Customer Attraction in the Digital Age

One of the major changes that characterizes the digital age is the path a brand or business has to follow in order to initiate a marketing dialog with its existing and potential consumers.

This route is called: **EMF – Effective Marketing Flow**

Digital culture requires us to start the journey with a very precise definition of our target audience, a characterized and clear micro-cluster, and then reach a level of familiarity with it, knowing its needs, its troubles, its expectations, its media consumption profile, its interests. We should be acquainted with its influential environment, the social groups to which it belongs, etc. This phase is based on the information expressed in the term: Social Intelligence.

The next step is a must – **creating relevant value for that specific target audience**. Once we get to know it, we should provide it with valuable content or tools to meet its expectations and needs at that very moment.

The way to do it right is by turning the brand or business into a content producer so that brands think like publishers. This is the most significant trigger for the growth of content-based marketing or Inbound Marketing.

Creating a personal or micro-segmental value will bring the brand closer to the listening stage which is perhaps the most problematic one in a digital environment, loaded with content, products, platforms and brands. Providing the right value at the right time will prepare the ground for listening. In the end, the competition for gaining the attention of consumers and customers is difficult and tight. Listening can lead to building a long-term relationship between the brand and its potential customers and / or preparing the grounds for a desirable market-to-market dialog.

Brands should understand:
that without acquaintance – there is no possibility of providing value. Without value – it is impossible to gain listening or a relationship without which there is no way to achieve effective marketing.

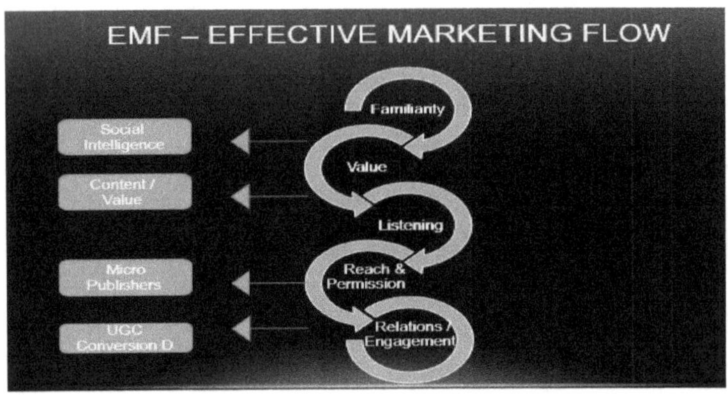
EMF – EFFECTIVE MARKETING FLOW
Familiarity
Value
Listening
Reach & Permission
Relations / Engagement
Social Intelligence
Content / Value
Micro Publishers
UGC Conversion D

Chapter Four

The Role of the Marketing Executive in the Digital Age

Traditional functions such as marketing managers and creative talents are about to drastically change in the next few years. Strategic thinking, creativity, media buying skills etc. – all these are not sufficient anymore.

The new leaders have to implement a long tail perception, and for that they need to have a new, fresh and complex set of skills:

1. A deep understanding of content creation / curation and content distribution.
2. Understanding the new field called SPOQ – Social Proof Of Quality. This new term refers to all types of people's reviews, recommendations, shared experiences and post-purchase feedback. SPOQ leads the new layer of Social Shopping (Products & Services) where the impact of other people on our purchasing decisions is much more

significant than advertising. New leaders need to know how to be involved and influence this exciting area of activity.

3. Knowing how to match micro-activity with the right audience.
4. Understanding big data output and handling the right marketing, product and business decisions based on that.
5. Direct the relevant team to focus on creating only five-second videos, not longer.
6. The ability to convert friends / followers to customers, as well as converting customers to brand promoters.
7. Understanding the importance of creating relations with micro-segments that are relevant to the brand.
8. Implement a work plan with Influencers and micro-Influencers, which is the main key for the success of any communication process.
9. Building and measuring a long tail-cross platform activity.
10. Understanding the basics and importance of the NMM field – Non-Media Marketing.

11. Building a set of real value for users.
12. Implementing a ROMI perception (Return on Marketing Investment) – even if you are a creative guy.
13. Lose old habits... and media vehicles that the audience is not familiar with and cannot provide you with Social Intelligence.
14. Use voice technology including voice search – which is going to lead the marketing industry.
15. Build fast brands. Leaders should know how to build quick relationships (consumers understand their benefits and value), they should find the right product UI that enables fast / quick navigation options. If you are in the E-com business, you should understand the importance of fast purchase (zero or one click purchasing) and quick delivery. Leaders should also be aware of the post-purchase stage. Important things such as quick response (customer relations) should be at the top of the priority list.
16. Use light technologies to support your brand's innovation image.

17. Visualize your message. If you use text messages, turn them into snackable content – short and valuable.

18. High analytical ability that allows changing work plans and activities on the move based on platform and campaign performance.

19. Understanding technologies that enable the differentiation of markets and products (marketology – the combination of market thinking with technological knowhow – will no longer be theoretical).

20. The traditional marketing managers were accustomed to talking **to** the customers. Not **with** the customers. Certainly not to work, day after day, on creating and maintaining relationships with existing and potential consumers. The unidirectional format of marketing-advertising activity has passed away from the world. This is a crucial change for most of the veteran marketers. The digital generation (those born to digital in the early 1980s) is impervious to market moves that are not based on familiarity-value-listening-authorization relationship.

21. The marketing manager in the digital age should adopt concepts of business development – developing a network of collaborations with content partners, technology partners, distribution partners and the like, a marketing activity based on the concept of a "long tail". It is impossible to succeed without building an open marketing plan of cooperation with factors that may have been seen in the past as a threat or potential competition.

22. Marketing professionals should listen to their customers and learn from them; allow them a foothold in the marketing process and in building products and content. The digital consumer is looking to be active, involved and influential.

23. Organizational structure and personnel. The new marketing manager is responsible for creating an organizational structure that meets the needs of the modern era – content managers, community managers, product managers, analysts, technologists and cultural and community researchers.

Chapter Five

What does the new digital marketing manager's dashboard look like?

Micro Clusters planning dashboard

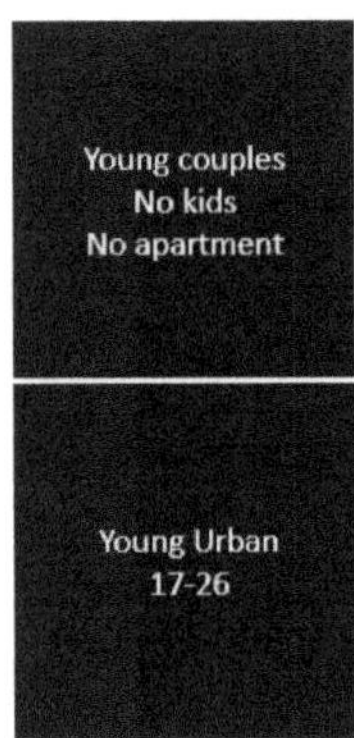

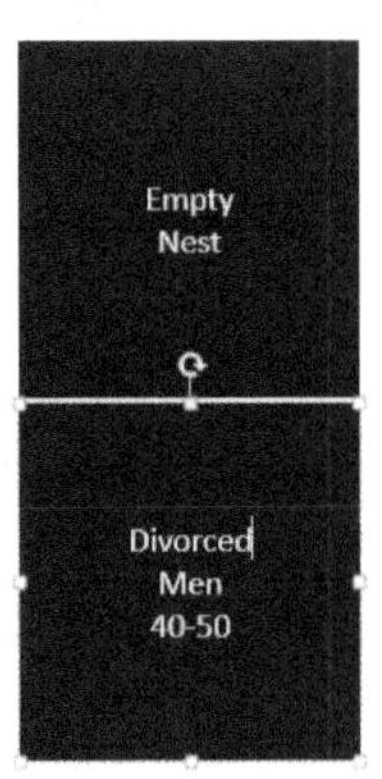

The marketing manager no longer prepares work plans for a target audience or a segment. The digital age requires marketers to work on **micro**-segments. The company should learn about each of its relevant clusters or tribes, recognize their characteristics – who they are, what motivates them, what their needs are, who influences them, whom they influence, what their media consumption profile is, what their general media consumption profile is, etc.

After having a detailed and targeted introduction plan, a penetration, persuasion and marketing outline can be prepared for each micro-cluster, based on the following components:

1. Advertising activity – campaigns
2. Organic search engine promotion activity
3. Establishing brand arenas on social networks (separately for each micro-segment)
4. Content activity – blog, presence on forums if relevant
5. Establishing mobile activities including apps, chatbots, and promotion in stores
6. Establishing e-commerce activity if necessary
7. Public relations including guerilla activity
8. Construction of moving products and value packages for each micro-cluster

Micro Cluster tactical plan

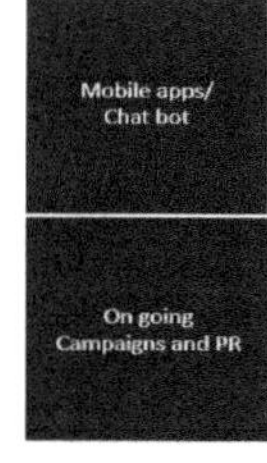

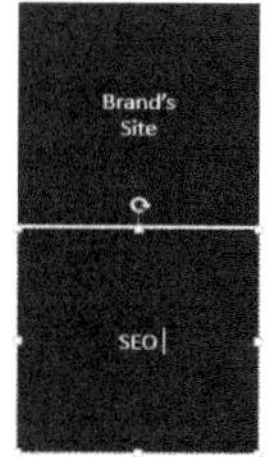

The digital marketing manager implements a Micro Approach triangle.

Micro-Cluster – Micro-Publishers – Micro-budgets

Everything is quantifiable, measurable, everything is accurate, diverse marketing processes, which require an intelligent analytical system and optimization while on the move.

Note – digital change is not a revolution but is rather a percolative process – a slippage on a timeline waiting for the tipping point.

The Tipping Point

We are at the threshold of that turning point – the millennial generation, followed by the Z generation, will soon be staffing marketing management. When this happens, we will witness the real changes in the world of marketing and advertising. Changes that will make a large number of the players in the industry irrelevant.

Chapter Six

The Passionate Segment

Strategic methodology in marketing and e-commerce

During the many years of digital activity, marketers have been dealing with the targeting issue. The first and fundamental question was – what audience I should focus on in order to ensure a good **Return on Marketing Investment – ROMI**. Professionals whom we have met over the past few years expressed concern that even in the current digital age – seemingly quantified and accurate – investing in marketing is not necessarily done efficiently and economically.

The Passionate Segment

This is a new segment underlining a new work concept that will change the marketing world in the coming years. It is a new approach which attempts to address the issue by concentrating all activities on one segment. The Passionates are people who are especially keen about a certain category (not about any specific brand but the entire category). For example, people who are passionate about cosmetics, fashion, health, soccer, cars, natural products, electronics and gadgets, etc.

This focused methodology dedicates every cent of the brand's marketing budget solely to this one segment. They will spread the word. Why? Because that is what passionate people do.

What are the reasons for directing all our marketing resources to this segment?

1. This target audience will try your products.
2. They also have the best chances to become returning customers.
3. The Passionates will read your content.
4. They will follow your social network activities and pages.
5. They will distribute your content (this is a field they are passionate about).
6. Your category Passionates will always be open to purchase new products – with reduced price sensitivity.
7. It will be much easier to make them your brand and product promoters. Provided that you recognize their value and create a good relationship with them.

How do you locate this audience?

It's easy – through targeted social media and search engine campaigns (Facebook and

Google have all the required intelligence on the passionate people), and of course by simple technological means that we can implement in our sites and through them learn about the interests of the surfers.

So, if you are active in the areas that are relevant to your Passionates and / or in e-commerce, **it is time to:**

Implement a Passionate Segment First strategy.

Dedicate your efforts to building your "Passionates' cluster" which is attracted to your category and set up a series of product offers with added value. It'll pay off.

Chapter Seven

Five Essential Steps in Digital Product Development

Effective digital marketing requires brands and companies to create their digital presence spider. These are the digital products through which the company will create a relationship with its customers, and which will also be the platform on which the brand will be built.

The following are the steps for setting up these digital products:

The idea – you should start with a requirements document (what you wish the product / application to do), including defining the development phases of the idea – must have / nice to have.

Market research and a competition comparison table – include reviews of similar products, performance data / where they operate / success / possible causes of success or failure of similar products in the world.

Go-No-Go phase – based on what you already know – argue the advisability of continuing the move.

Main trigger to use – ask yourself, what will make people want to use your product? This part can include one or more of the following features:

- Basic need
- Stress-free life
- Savings – Money / Time
- Fun
- Community
- Social connections
- Enrichment / information
- Personal empowerment

Product Specification – Which features will be included in the app / site? What content will the project focus on? How will these features be available to the user? In what order of use? What will be the usage flow?

Development – Choose 2-3 development providers – a tender between development factors based on professionalization parameters, experience, portfolio, service, schedules, price.

Package / UI / UX
Beta – marketing test – test the product with a focus group and effective measurement tools.

Soft launch – for a defined audience and a reasonable marketing budget.

Post-performance review – technical performance evaluation, usage performance, user feedback.

Market penetration Plan – Implementing a full GTM – Go-To-Market plan including analytics and measuring.

Beyond these necessary stages, there are **four anchors necessary for the design of a digital product**. These anchors should be implemented at the outset planning and characterization stage. Without them, it will be difficult to achieve market-business success.

Product planning: Social Intelligence & Big data

A digital product that does not know its users cannot succeed. A digital product that does not collect information about its customers cannot maintain efficient product-market planning. At the product planning stage, ask yourself how you can build user and customer profiles.

To that end, spread "information collection buttons" throughout the product usage flow – from its registration stage and gather information from dialog boxes or customer benefits. All this information should be set up in your cloud so that you can use it for your planning purpose, product planning, marketing and business offers to your customers based on what you have learned about them.

Focus: Usage frequency

Have an idea for a new product / application / site? At the planning stage you should already ask yourself: what do you predict will be the average usage frequency of your application or product? Usage frequency is a central factor, a key indicator of success or failure. If the frequency of use is less than twice a week in most categories, you should question the feasibility of your venture.

Built-in targeting: Micro-clusters

Launching a product that "speaks to everyone" is not a good Idea in the digital field.

You should implement micro-clusters thinking – the digital age marks the end of the mass marketing approach. Any new product has to be developed and designed with clear characteristics of micro-segmentation. This is a process in which the entrepreneur knows his precise audience – its anxieties, needs, expectations, what motivates it, what irritates it, what characterizes its social environment, what its social and economic abilities are, etc.

Micro-segment is more accurate, more efficient and truer when it comes to digital marketing. For example, the micro-segment of first pregnancy women share the same needs, the same worries, the same fears, expectations and desires. Once you are able to recognize all of that, it is easier to communicate with them, connect with them, and develop a long-term relationship with them. All these factors should be part of the product planning stage.

Clear Business models

Planning to set out with a new digital initiative, you should already know what your business model is at the product design stage. Choosing a business model, in other words, what you are going to make a living from, is a decision that needs to be made at the initial stage, because it bears implications on the product content, and its design.

There are five main business models:
Advertising – in this model, the product / application is free and the project takes place through the connection to advertising sources – usually programmatic advertising.
Freemium – this model allows free use of basic features, and add-ons of content or applications for a fee.
Subscription – a large number of publishers and content players in the world are moving or are considering switching to this model which opens all the content to a user for a monthly subscription fee.
License – product or technology provided to companies / customers in return for a fee / a license fee based on the number of users/ multiple uses per license unit.
Transactions – in this model, the company

receives part of the sales revenue. For example, an online shopping mall that sells third party fashion products will receive a percentage of every sale they make.

While planning your digital product think about Differentiation

You should draw a competition table based on comparing your product to the competing ones already on the market. It is advisable to specify your product as much as possible, in order to understand whether it is better or poorer than the others. That will help you decide your company's USP – unique selling proposition, or in other words on a clear picture of your product advantage, which in turn could define your marketing and communication strategy. Your product could differentiate in the features layer and / or packaging layer, and / or in the way you are going to the market.

The digital consumer – who is he and how is he changing the traditional marketing world

Generation Z and the millennials were born into digital and its features affect the way we do marketing. This generation holds close to 40% of the workforce and in its interaction with brands and media it demands influence and involvement, it displays poor loyalty (workplace / brand) and expects an immediate response to its needs – "I want it and I want it now."

Sometimes they call this young generation Generation C – as in Connected.

They are simultaneous consumers of multiple media / platforms, which means we're in a continuous struggle for their attention. This generation is sometimes called Generation D – as in Dislike.

With poor loyalty and high expectation for significant value from a brand / advertiser / marketer, these digital natives ask for total control over information consumption, transparency, personalization and impact on content and processes. The digital consumer moves from passivity to collaboration, which is also expressed in sharing content and experiences – he can be a loud critic and thus bury a product or service yet similarly can also be a wonderful and authentic promoter of the company's products and brand. The digital user has zero tolerance for an average usage experience; thus, brands should be committed not only to content but also to user experience.

The young consumer is not loyal to any one buying venue – he shops everywhere. With the power moving to the consumer, local stores no longer need to compete only with local competitors. The young consumer has more alternatives and less free time. He knows how much he is willing to spend and how to get it.

Digital consumers move between platforms

and are hard to locate – so, where are they? Sites, social networks, mobile, smart TV and wearable computers. Our message needs to be relevant, personal and decomposed, "chewed", clear and easy and be out there on all these platforms.

The digital consumer thinks visually – leaning towards image thinking and dialog, which requires the assimilation of a new / digital aesthetics. Among others, a combination of "quiet" technology – one that is not at the center of the interaction with the consumer yet provides value and simplifies usage for the benefit of the consumer. No wonder that Instagram is the fastest growing network among brands – 77% of the top 100 brands have marketplaces on Instagram.

Chapter Eight

The Most Important Segment of Your Marketing Activity

The saying in the media and brand world claims that the people you most need will leave you first, and then the rest will follow. I guess that the first to leave / let go of the traditional media tools, as well as the digital publishers, are the millennials and generation Z.

The US industry is currently witnessing a revolution. For the first time, the millennials have become the largest demographic segment, and in terms of business potential, they are more significant than the X and the baby generation.

Let's redraw these generations' map, in terms of marketing and media:

Baby boomers – born between 1946 and1964. This generation is associated with the age of plenty – they were the first to be born to home television and witnessed the initial entry of technology into the average house.

The X Generation – born from the early 60s to the end of the 70s of the 20th century. This generation, unlike its predecessors, spends much more time at home and therefore is exposed to a multitude of media channels and marketing messages.

The Y Generation – the Millennials. Born in the 80s and 90s of the 20th century, they are the digital natives, who have been exposed to global stimuli from an early age: music, fast food, global news broadcasts, the internet and so on. They have no qualms when it comes to returning to live at their parents' home even as grownups. They also average seven jobs by the age of thirty and marry late.

The Z Generation – born to 4-5 screens – computer, TV, smartphone, tablet, laptop. A technological, visual and involved generation, which is more digital, more calculated, more apt to online purchasing – primarily mobile shopping, but still has, compared to the Millennials, limited purchasing capability. In a few years, they are going to become more significant.

Therefore, the Millennials – the first generation born to digital – is the most important one for brands and media companies. They, as well as the following generation, present a different and elusive consumer profile – less linear television, less loyalty to brands, sharing products and content, impatient and intolerant of unpleasant buying experiences, and requirement for interaction and involvement.

These two younger generations are similar in terms of the difficulty they pose to brands and media companies, but still differ significantly.

Pay close attention to the following differences:

The Z Generation is not just a sophisticated content consumer but also a content producer. Most of the successful Influencers belong to this generation. Generation Z, more than the millennial one, was born to online shopping (primarily mobile). It, more than any other generation, has adopted and demands visual communication.

Amazon, for example, studied this segment and launched Amazon TEENS – a platform that allows its young audience to shop with its own personal budget. The service and the way Amazon promotes it were influenced by a recent HRC study which showed that 61% of screen-purchasing decisions are influenced by friends, with 13% by bloggers. Most of these youth are not influenced by traditional advertising and use social networks while shopping.

The millennials and the Z generation are the segments you should invest your money in. They do not spend time in the areas where most marketing managers invest in, and do not wait for celebrities to tell them what to buy. One other important point – the millennials are the new leaders. They are the ones sitting in the drivers' seat now (or very soon). From here, the real change will begin with the implementation of smarter, more accurate and measurable digital marketing programs. **The end of spray and pray.**

Chapter Nine

The Age of Big Brands' Market Share Erosion

Small players can use the digital space for closing gaps

One of the strategic marks of the digital industry might happen with tectonic movements to narrow the gaps between brands and small businesses, big brands and companies. This is not going to happen all at once and not in all categories, but it is already budding in areas such as fashion, food, financial services and consulting.

Why is it feasible to expect an erosion in the market share of large brands in the future?

1. Small Business-Friendly Promotion Platforms – Google and Facebook – consider the SMB segment as their main growth engine for the next few years, so they invest resources and creativity to get these businesses to use their promotion platforms. These platforms enable every business, with

any budget, to create a presence and generate leads for sales.

2. All marketing activity is leaning towards focusing on micro-segments, where big brands do not enjoy any significant advantage. In addition, micro-budget marketing is more efficient than huge, expensive campaigns.
3. Sales platforms like Amazon do not discriminate between large and small in terms of presence and market efficiency. Amazon's promotion and presence mechanisms are available to any business owner or brand, enabling them to locate their target audience and create a relevant proposition for it.
4. The Z and Y generation – digital natives – is not characterized by high brand loyalty.
5. Digital marketing is based on relations with potential consumers. Marketing managers of some major brands have yet to internalize the change in the nature of the marketing dialog.
6. Branding and positioning, which in the past were based on massive brand marketing activity, are now concentrating on creating consumers' involvement and turning them into brand promoters. The main term in branding

and positioning is Emotional Engagement.
When it comes to Emotional Engagement, a small brand that works against a micro-segment has often the advantage of understanding customers, producing value, retaining customers by developing a rewarding digital relationship, and creating a true dialog that reaches a significant level of attention.

7. Small businesses have often been established or run by digital natives who are more hands-on in digital marketing than their large competing companies. These young people also quickly adopt new technologies and platforms. For example: visual search, voice services, integration of technologies such as virtual reality and blockchain / crypto-based solutions in marketing programs, and, of course, collaborations with relevant Influencers in their category.
8. Automation in the development of platforms and products. Today you no longer need huge budgets to set up and launch applications, sites, chatbots, and other digital features.

What do small brands need in order to accelerate market erosion?

Implementing a micro-segmentation strategy based on micro-publishers /micro budget.

- The assimilation of differentiation technologies is yet to be found in the Blue Ocean regions – visual search, voice search, blockchain, etc. Big brands will move in these directions much more slowly.
- Collaborations with relevant influential teams.
- Specialization in launching and selling products and services on Amazon.
- Collaborations with corresponding small businesses. It is also possible to establish a local network of small businesses that support each other in promoting and expanding supply (packages).
- Investment in communities of committed consumers – preferably focus on the most important segment – the Passionates of the category. They will make the difference between branding activity and positioning of small and large brands.

Chapter Ten

DPQ – Digital Presence Quality

A tool for measuring the quality of the digital presence of brands

In the digital marketing age, digital presence of brands and companies is a prerequisite for creating relationships, which are the basics for effective marketing. A cross-platform digital presence enables the brand to be part of the consumers' life and create an ongoing dialog with them, based on familiarity and social intelligence. That will help brands to provide consumers with their relevant needed value.

This marketing stage is much more important and effective than campaign waves. Therefore, and in order to improve this strategic step, it is advisable to use simple tools for comparative tracking of the brand's digital presence comparing it to its competitors. One of the simplest and most effective tools is: **DPQ – Digital Presence Quality**.

DPQ is a comparative table that tracks the brand's monthly performance as well as its various activities on all relevant platforms: social, home site, mobile features, blog, etc. It compares all brand data to that of at least three relevant competitors at the end of each month.

What are the relevant factors of this tool?

Social Networks – is where we follow friends, followers, Engagement Index and other activities.
Mobile – we measure app downloads, uses, users and engagement actions (comments, shares, SPOQ etc.).
The brand's homepage – is where we perform a monthly comparison of visits, visitors, bounce rate, and average time spent on the site.
Blog – if the company has an active blog (highly recommended), we will follow bloggers, readers and engagement (sharing, comments, etc.).
Monthly Trends – is where we perform the monthly summary of trends for each platform – which trends went up, which trends weakened, and how significant the gaps are.
MUC – Monthly Users Change – the monthly fluctuations in absolute numbers for each player on each platform.
Budget / MUC – The monthly budget to total change ratio in the number of new people exposed to our digital product (across all platforms). This budgetary figure allows us to understand the market's ROI over the past month in terms of strengthening the user base involved in the brand's digital assets.

Action Items – Based on the monthly quantitative tracking, a marketing plan is drawn up for the next month – which competitor to focus on, how to allocate the marketing budget, which platform needs support and which can attract the rest of the company's digital spider, etc.

DPQ – Digital Presence Quality
(monthly)

		Your Brand	Competitor A	Competitor B	Competitor C	Monthly trends
Social (Per Each *social network*)	**Followers / Friends**					
	SPOQ Social Proof of Quality (Comments, Share etc.)					
Mobile	**Installs**					
	Active Users					
	Mobile SPOQ					
Site	**Monthly Visitor**					
	Bounce Rate					
	Time On Site					
Blog	**Users**					
	SPOQ					
MUC Monthly Users Change	**Per Platform**					
Monthly Budget Divided by MUC	**Total**					

Chapter Eleven

SFT- Strategic Focus Table. How can you use this tool to improve your plans?

Digital marketing consists of many factors. Some essential, others less. Depending on what category your brand belongs to. Multiple elements and the endless variety of channels and platforms raise questions regarding company's focus, directions and budget allocation:

How much should you invest in each platform, should you implement a Mobile First Strategy that requires a significant investment in an app's promotion and retention? Which segment should you focus on? Should you be involved in the fundamental domain called **SPOQ – Social Proof of Quality**? (This important marketing channel refers to all types of people, reviews, recommendations, shared experiences and post-purchase feedback.) Does your media strategy need to focus on traditional advertising or maybe be more focused on methodological work with Influencers and Micro-Influencers?

Such questions and others should be part of the marketing professional's set of considerations.

The answers to these questions form the basis of the outline of your marketing strategy. Naturally, each category and each company have different answers to these questions.

A simple **Strategic Focus Table** may help you to get the right answers.

For example, there are categories in which decision-making is not affected by traditional advertising. In these categories, people's experience, reviews and recommendations have significantly more impact on a consumer's decision to buy products and services. In these categories, Content Marketing also plays a significant role in users' decisions.

Categories such as health, education, personal services (designers, lawyers, trainers, psychological etc.), travel, pharma, online shopping etc. should favor **many-to-many marketing (SPOQ)** and **Content Marketing** and neglect traditional advertising.

So, if you are a player in these categories, your Go-To-Market plan should be based on SPOQ and Content Marketing.

Another example:

Companies in the areas of retail, convenience stores, groceries, travel, leisure and online shopping should implement a **Mobile First Strategy**.

Implementing this demanding strategy is considered to be a significant commitment but it comes with a huge reward (if you succeed in becoming a part of your users' everyday life by having a real presence on people's mobile device).

You are welcome to use this **Strategic Focus Table** before building yourself an effective and budget plan.

Strategic Focus Table

	Mobile First strategy	Content	SPOQ	Search	Ecomm	Passionate segment	Traditional Advertising	Micro Publishers
Grocery	V				V			
Pharma		V	V	V	V	V		V
Health		V	V	V	V	V		V
Beauty		V		Request	V	V	V	V
Personal Services & Products		V	V	V	V			V
Travel	V	V	V	V	V	V		V
leisure	V	V	V		V	V		
Education		V	V		V			V
Finance		V	V		V	V		V
Media & Content		V			V		V	
CPG				Request	V		V	
Retail	V				V		V	
On Line Retail	V	V	V	V	V	V		
Automotive		V				V	V	
Real Estate				V			V	
Home Products				V	V		V	

Chapter Twelve

Most effective marketing vehicles according to consumer's perception

A cross-category research (ROMI Media, Research division, 2019) measured the impact of several marketing vehicles on people's consumption decisions in main categories / industries.

The research was focused on four main vehicles:

1. **SPOQ – Social Proof of Quality**. This vehicle is based on users' reviews and combines sentiment and volume of user recommendations. Ranking products and services by users' recommendation will be a leading factor in the next phase of Digital Marketing.
2. **Content Marketing.** Brands and services provide consumers with relevant high value content and consequently develop ongoing relations with the audience.

3. **UIA – Users' Initiated Advertisements**. The commercial information is initiated by users' search for a specific product or service.
4. **ATL / One to Many Advertisements.** This is a traditional mass media, commercial interaction, in which one source (brand, company, service provider) tries to convince its audience to choose its product or service. This vehicle refers to offline or digital ads such as TV, magazines, radio, websites and social ads, etc.

The research focused on 12 main categories:

Grocery

Pharma

Health care

Beauty

Convenience stores

Personal services (lawyers, accountants, etc.)

Travel

Leisure

Education

Finance

Media & Content

CPG

Retail

Online Retail

Automotive

Real estate

Home Products

Personal products

Research results

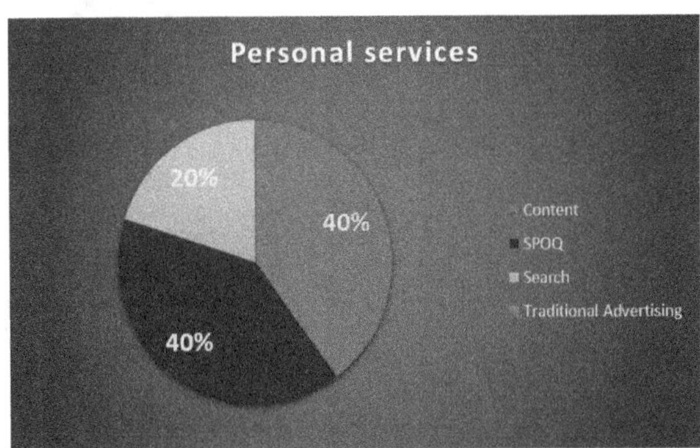

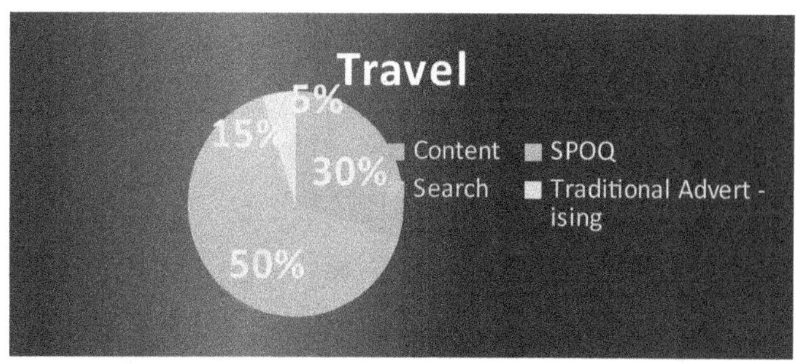
Travel
5%
15%
30%
50%
Content
SPOQ
Search
Traditional Advert -
ising

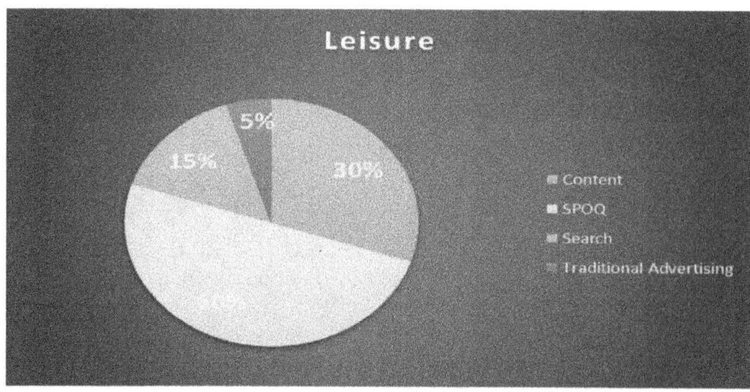
Leisure
5%
15%
30%
Content
SPOQ
Search
Traditional Advertising

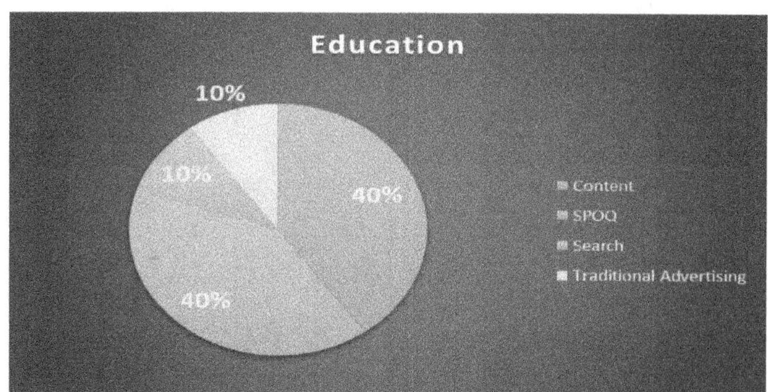
Education
10%
10%
40%
40%
Content
SPOQ
Search
Traditional Advertising

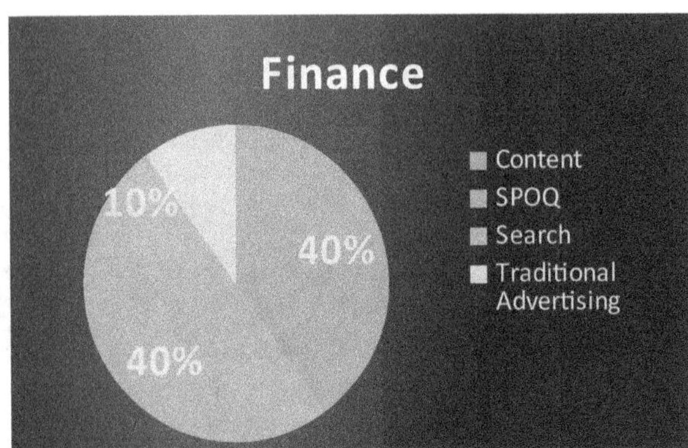
Finance
10%
40%
40%
Content
SPOQ
Search
Traditional Advertising

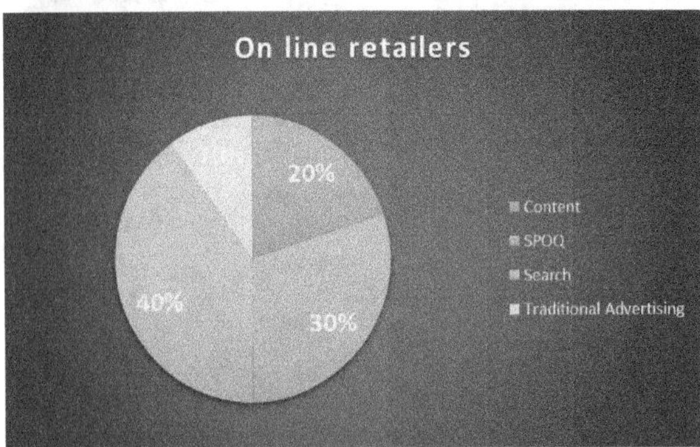
On line retailers
20%
40%
30%
Content
SPOQ
Search
Traditional Advertising

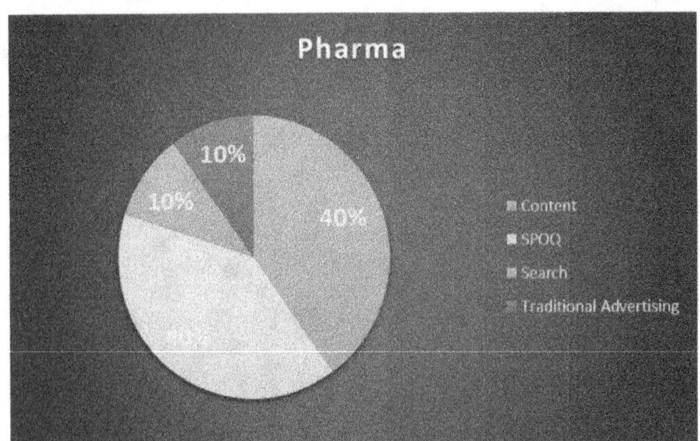
Pharma
10%
10%
40%
Content
SPOQ
Search
Traditional Advertising

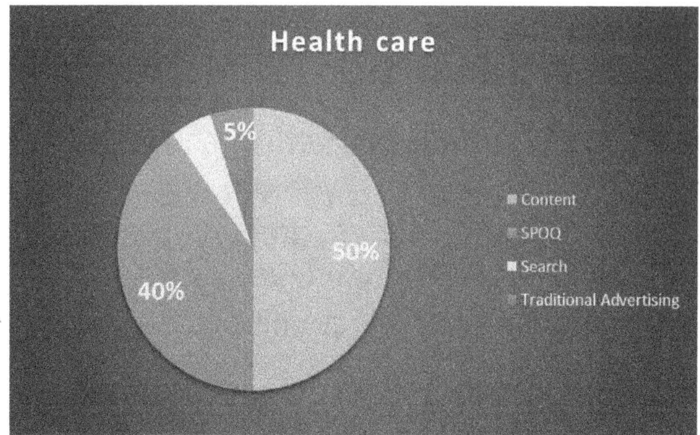

The research's main conclusions

In some of the categories, traditional advertising was found to have no impact.

SPOQ – Social Proof of Quality vehicle has major impact on people when they have to take decisions in the fields of leisure, travel, consumer services (such as lawyers, coaches, psychologists, dieticians and accountants), education, healthcare, online retail, pharma and finance. It seems that in these categories, one should invest one's entire marketing budget in the evolving discipline of SPOQ and Content and avoid any One-To-Many / ATL activity.

According to this research, **traditional advertising** makes an impact and should be the leading marketing vehicle in the Consumers Package goods.

UIA / Search engine marketing should be included in your activity if you are active in the categories of online stores, grocery, personal products, CPG, real estate and automotive finance, software and electronics.

This research may help marketers choose what vehicles will lead their marketing plan according to their main category. Traditional advertising should play only a minor role in some of the high involvement category (products and services) activities.

Chapter Thirteen

Prepare yourself for the next generation of advertising

Five key trends that will lead the digital advertising industry in the coming years

The advertising industry is in turmoil, and all of those involved admit as much – traditional advertising agencies, digital organizations, media companies, content producers who make their living from advertising, and of course, the brands that are struggling for the attention of consumers and potential customers.

In order to prepare for the coming years, one should pay attention to five trends on five levels of activity: technology, consumer acquisition channels, advertising formats, targeting and focus areas.

Technology: Programmatic

The rapid transition to programmatic advertising is one of the major changes which affects the advertising industry and will continue to do so in the coming years. Everything is done automatically without the need for a sales dialog. Campaigns are based on real-time bidding technologies. To date, about 75% of digital campaigns in the US are programmatic.

These technologies will continue to lead the industry, and spread to its other parts, such as smart television advertising and billboards.

Channels: Influencers/ Micro-Media

Mass Marketing / Spray and Pray – These terms will soon be obsolete with the industry currently embracing accurate, more effective, measurable media that reinforce terms such as:

Emotional Engagement

These are micro-publishers – Influencers, bloggers and public opinion leaders on social networks, individuals who have become influential and effective media vehicles. If you are a small fashion designer and wish to reach a target audience relevant to your new collection or line of products, there is no need to invest in advertising on major platforms, sites, TV channels or billboards. Collaborating with a blogger or relevant gatekeepers can expose your products to tens of thousands of potential customers with a high attention index. What characterizes the relationship between these Influencers / micro-Influencers and their followers is listening. They listen to their blogger or their social leader. Listening – something you would not be able to get by advertising on major sites or on television. These are the newest, most effective and measurable media.

Format: Snackable Ads

The most important audience in the digital age are the two generations born to digital: **Generations Y & Z**
If you want to present them with an idea, product or service, you should come up with a way to do it in five to seven seconds – not easy, but possible. Agencies need to combine creativity and functionality. There are currently creative agencies around the world who specialize in producing and distributing snackable ads.

Targeting: The Passionate Segment
Targeting is also changing, launching a new radical path. More brands are about to focus on the most effective segment – the **Passionates** of their category. We know them: the fashion, sports, riding freaks, those who will not miss any natural health product, or those hungry for new electronic gadgets.

The Passionates will try your products. They will talk about your products, read your blog, be your Facebook friends and send your posts to theirs. This segment will become your brand's best promoters. They will research your brand content and value, share with their friends, and more likely be the ones to initiate discussions about your brand and products.

This segment will bring you the best ROMI – Return on Marketing Investment.

Focus: Consumer's value / Inbound marketing

As for the brand's messages, the advertising industry is also reorganizing itself. Brands should minimize promises and brand stories and shift their creativity toward content that generates **value** for the target audience. This is sometimes called **selling without selling**, a relationship based on giving. One that at a certain point also prepares the ground for a sales dialog.

Chapter Fourteen

Advertising Products – The Next Generation

New technologies and the changes in content consumption habits are witnessing a dramatic impact on advertising. Non-targeted banners, linear TV ads, newspaper ads are going to be replaced by smart advertising products that will enable brands to create an effective marketing dialog with relevant audiences.

The new generation advertising products use popular platforms that are becoming part of our daily lives:

1. Personal Voice Services

Voice search is becoming more accessible and popular. It is a friendly application, easy to use and reliable.

This platform collects unique information about us based on linking the virtual assistant to our household appliances such as our fridge, for example; it gathers useful data – the type of products our family uses, our consumption rate of the products, shopping dates etc. These platforms open their doors to advertisers and offer new and attractive advertising products.

Advertising products that feature these platforms:

Intention-Based Ad
An advertising product that is connected to the consumers' buying intention, based on their purchasing history and data.
Ad per need
An advertising product based on information about products that are usually purchased and are currently missing in the fridge.
Interests-Based Ad
Information stored on the basis of consumption habits of the virtual assistant users is translated into consumption profiles – consumption of content, information, entertainment and products.

2. **Segmented Audio Services**

A Podcast is (usually) a radio program broadcast on the Internet. A podcast usually consists of a sequence of programs and / or episodes and / or chapters. The beauty is that it can be listened to anytime, anywhere and on any device. In terms of marketing and media strategy, a podcast is the ultimate format of micro-publisher. It is usually managed by a person passionate for a certain category, who has set up a "radio station" and turns to a clearly defined, not very large audience, which is also passionate about the same category. This format features loyalty, involvement, repeated listening and a detailed and clear listeners' profile – in short, the ultimate dream of every marketer.

67% of Americans over the age of 13 listen to podcasts. 22% do it on mobile. 85% listen to the entire program (or almost). The cost of advertising on the majority of podcasts is one of the highest in the industry, and advertisers understand the power of loyalty and involvement on this intimate format. Podcasts are one of the few ad formats that are well targeted and naturally integrate into the broadcast. The ultimate configuration (ads that fit into the consumer's experience) of native advertisements.

Advertising products that feature in these platforms:

Micro cluster native and interests-based ads

3. Personal Communication Platforms

Messaging platforms meet the personal and immediate need of consumers to communicate. Advertisers who find the right way to join the dialog between people will meet the first and fundamental goal of every marketing move – **listening**. As long as it is done in an elegant, non-intrusive manner, which provides value to the customer, based on familiarity with his needs.

Advertising on Messenger provides higher CTR.

Clicking data on ads is considered the highest compared to any other platform. These performances are based on the advertiser's ability to engage the participants in a way that does not interfere with their activity. Today there are more than 15 messaging platforms around the world with more than 150 million users each. These platforms maintain a ratio of MAU / DAU, (Monthly Active Users/ Daily Active Users ratio) which is the best in the media. The combination of high frequency of use and the ability to accurately target makes messaging platforms one of the most effective tools for marketing dialog.

Advertising products that feature these platforms:
Micro-cluster native and snackable ads.
It is an amazing advertising vehicle as long as brands take into consideration the needs of the users. In other words, short ads that fit the user's experience.

Chapter Fifteen

How should you promote your business with video?

Do you have a new or an existing product? Need to promote your company? Do you wish to invest in your personal branding?

Video is the ultimate solution for you, no matter if you are a big company, a famous brand or a small player.

Why video?

- Virality – video is the most shared format.

- Production value / quality is not an issue anymore – anyone can do it.

- YouTube is an optimal platform for closing gaps between small and big players.

- Google will reward players who are also active on YouTube.

1. How to start? Brief – for a work plan

A video campaign will begin with detailed planning that includes the following elements:

- Product description including its advantages, strengths and weaknesses compared to the competitors.
- Defining the target audience – the more accurately the target audience is defined, the more efficient the move will be.
- Pyramid of advantages – rating key advantages.
- A message pyramid – which 2-3 of your product advantages should the marketing activity focus on?
- Goals and targets – defining quantitative and qualitative goals.

2. <u>Defining the target audience</u>

This is no longer just a basic definition. In the digital age it is necessary to define your target audience in a precise and detailed manner:

What interests them?

Who are their friends?

Which platforms do they use?

What is their digital profile?

Which social groups are they active in?

What do they believe in?

What do they trust?

What are they afraid of?

Whom do they love?

What are they looking for?

What are they talking about?

Who influences them?

Whom do they influence?

3. Setting the environment and the nature of the video

At this stage we will characterize the physical environment of video production –

Background? Atmosphere? Equipment? (Professional tools indicate a large company but are definitely not necessary). The nature of the video? Emotional / Productive / Informational (statistics, market surveys, etc.).

4. The clip's typology

At this stage we will produce a script for each of the stages of the product promotion: the introductory stage, the uniqueness stage in which we describe the advantages of our product, the concrete proposing stage of the brand, and finally the relationship stage (invitation to be in touch through the company's social activities).

5. **Strategy for producing clips**

What will be the best video clip for each stage?

Multilayer video that includes more than one stage?

Producing three types of creative for each stage – the law of diminishing returns is valid here – the effect of each clip or creative diminishes over time, at which point it is advisable to come up with a new script.

6. **What do they measure? KPIs – Key Performance Indicators**
    - Subscribers
    - Engagement Index = Like/Views > 1%
    - Correlation between subscribers' number and average views
    - SPOQ (Social Proof of Quality), in other words – how many people and what do they have to say about your content? SPOQ Index is based on sentiment and volume of reviews

7. **The content mix strategy should be based on four anchors:**
    1. Original content – which takes into account the advantages of the platform's distribution (YouTube, Facebook, Instagram, SnapChat etc.).
    2. Evergreen content – content that can be relevant for a long time.

3. Snackable Content – short, concentrated content for those who tend to prefer short, chewed and packaged content.
4. UGC – All content should invite users / viewers to add something of their own – comments, sharing experiences. The company should build the channel and content to allow significant room for users' contribution.

SPOQ – Social Proof of Quality

8. <u>Your video channel distribution strategy should be based on four anchors:</u>

- **Detachable channels** – Dissembling channels – break up pieces of the company's content and spread them on different platforms, where you can reach a dialog with your desired target audience.
- **Viral distribution – your content should be sharable** – you should focus on a content that generates a trigger for distribution with your audience (humor, playfulness, originality).
- **Organic distribution – your content should be searchable** – content creation, structure and nature should take into account the requirements of search engines.
- Paid Media – measurable and targeted campaigns on social networks can help, especially in the first stage of your YouTube channel.

The formula of a successful YouTube channel.

Tracking successful YouTube channels, a clear common formula stands out:

They are produced by the category's passionate content producers and are directed to content consumers that are passionate about the same category.

A passionate creator creates content for a passionate audience. For example: dancing, sandwich preparing artists, extreme trips.

Chapter Sixteen

No more than five seconds of advertisement

ComScore released research results that showed what we already suspected – the 30 / 20 seconds advertisement format is not relevant anymore.

While this is not necessarily true for all of us, it is certainly valid for the Y and Z generations, the digital generations, which are currently the most courted by most brands and services.

So what does it mean?

These young people, considered to be the most coveted audience by most brands and companies, have an ad patience of 5 seconds per ad tops.

This means that all those advertisers who have taken a movie that they made last year for their TV ad and pinned it on to YouTube made a wrong move. Or maybe their client was wrong when hiring their services.

So if you are young, creative and talented – a little more than your boss, it's time to set up a creative agency with one focused specialty: creating effective 5-second ads. For YouTube Ads can even be shown on TV's.

Chapter Seventeen

How will the digital currency technology affect the advertising and media industry?

The next revolution is on its way, the new technological player which came up with a new digital relationship means a digital token whose value is not determined by the value of a commodity or by one central body, but by an agreement between a network of users (Bitcoin, Ethereum Ripple, etc.).

This financial-marketing-business tool operates in an environment free of any central entity to supervise transactions, replaced by a set of computers that approves them. Confirmed transactions are sealed and encoded through an endless chain of blocks, which translates into a decentralized economic system – removing the financial control from the bankers.

Many tokens are already available today, attempting to come up with new relationship models for internet companies and users. Cryptocurrency will enable new business models based on a new win-win democratic model (not just companies such as Google and Facebook that earn their fees from content and users' engagement). In other words, we are about to take part in the new democratization, where the power from central entities that trade information is shifting to the information daily owners (the users).

Today, two main players are present in this field:

1. Crypto coins whose purpose is to preserve and transfer value (like Bitcoin).

2. Companies that offer content, shopping, information, community. Applications offering token-based new business models have added a layer of reward and user involvement based on the system's currency.

How does this affect the content area?
We will witness more and more marketing activities that use token micropayments-based solutions wishing to reward content producers for their input. These content platforms reward writers, content distributors and other community activists, in currencies. The format is simple: those with more tokens, have the highest significant impact on the site and consequently will be promoted, and their feedback heard more. The more active the more tokens you win (you can also buy tokens).

How does this affect communication?
The democratic system will make it possible to use means of communication such as non-centralized, non-supervised, non-managed messaging software, which does not gather information about us. The software requires token payments, but we get to keep our personal data.

How does this affect gaming?
Gaming platforms and applications are often based on the tendency of players to improve their experience by moving forwards to advanced levels and acquiring, on the move, add-ons and applications. This area is going to change to buying tokens with currency for accessories, extensions and add-ons for the game itself. The gaming field will become a buy-to-sell token-based marketplace with the option to exchange it for external currencies.

How does this affect advertising?
Advertising is in a predicament – advertisers have lost faith in the revenue they were supposed to get. Questions such as "how many people actually saw the ad or how many people are involved in the broadcasted ads?" cloud the continued relationship between brands, advertisers and media.
These questions might disappear with the proper assimilation of Blockchain-based solutions by implementing a system of

engagement and reward for people exposed to the ad. A user will receive a token every time he watches a commercial and the advertisers will receive accurate data on entries and engagement, and so will the brands be able to track their exact exposure.

How does this affect the media?

The publishers of recent years are battered and losing their business – they lose money (ads) to Google and social networks. They also lose loyal readers / users to the elusive social world.

The Blockchain-based range of currencies could be these media companies' salvation: more publishers will join micro-payment – a new token-based business model. Users will receive tokens as they spend more time on the site or reading an article and the tokens will start trading and produce revenue for both parties.

To conclude, Blockchain technology and digital currencies are great for content and media companies, advertisers and of course, consumers and users. This technological revolution will lead to a real upheaval of the media, advertising, content and communication. A real revolution that happens once every few decades. Media companies, publishers, advertisers and communication companies need to study the issue and create an updated strategy for the coming years.

Chapter Eighteen

Augmented Reality changes the dialog between consumers and brands

Augmented Reality technology has been with us for quite a few years, but it seems that now it is making a significant step towards integration into product-business-marketing. This technology uses reality as it is and can place objects in it in real time. The additional object layer can be animated, informative, in video or in any other format that expands what the user sees.

How can this technology be used?

- On the go offline business marketing – road signs, directions, information about businesses and restaurants, information on works of art in the museum, and the like.
- **Sale point marketing** – enables "live" interaction at the sale point while deepening the experience and utilizing the technology to provide the customer with more product

information before receiving the purchase application.

- **Interaction** between consumers and brands through a magazine or sale point.
- **Education** – interactive learning – the way to stimulate thinking, involvement, experience and curiosity goes through adding a layer of visual stimulation over the existing layer of reality in real time.
- Integrated gameplay – consumer involvement goes through games and inspirational experiences (like Pokémon, for example).

Augmented Reality technology and applications are changing the branding and consumer-brand dialog:

<u>Data Visualization</u>
Evidently, everything ultimately concentrates on data. This technology enables the visualization of data in favor of the consumer and the application operator.

Marketing & Product Visualization

This technology enables the product to be made available in a reality-wise way in order to enhance the experience of the pre-acquisition stage.

New way of brand storytelling – Experiential

Various layers of information and experience open up new creative possibilities at the brand's story stage and expand the way consumers connect to the brand and its environment.

Connecting people and brands by remote events

Augmented Reality applications allow the brand to reduce the distance between it and potential customers by creating "remote events touching" without the need to constantly bring the consumer to the point of sale.

Mobile device as an enabler

The big players have already developed the capabilities of Augmented Reality on your cellphone.

Functionality first

Augmented Reality will focus on the practical benefits to the consumer. This area is more stimulating because extraordinary excitement produces more information, is easier to use and understand, provides “tactile” products before purchasing,

enhances the shopping experience, and so on. This, we believe, is why Augmented Reality will become an effective tool for brands and marketers.

<u>The new age of live print</u>

Does this open the door to somewhat revive print? We believe so, marginally though. Segmented magazines know how to use this technology, wisely turning them interactive.

Chapter Nineteen

What will the new ad agency look like?

Anyone who is involved in the advertising industry understands (or will do so soon) that the place of traditional advertising agencies in the value chain is losing altitude and significance. Advertising agencies need to reinvent themselves or find another business.

So how will advertising agencies look in the coming years?
An advertising agency should build itself on three basic strengths:

Digital Centric Structure

Some advertising agencies still perceive the digital world as an effective place to run campaigns. Yet, real assimilation of digital thinking is called for – the Y and Z generations born to digital do not simply pop into properties and digital platforms. They live there. Advertising agencies should appreciate that they, too, need to join digital life and not just use it to promote their brand.

Full service and data-driven organization

Data is crucial for the continued existence of any advertising agency; therefore, it is definitely advisable to establish a department that is dedicated just to that. Nowadays, any advertising agency could use easy technologies available for implementing data centers within its systems and not to outsource it to an outside supplier!!!! Data is the driving force of any marketing-business success.

Performance & Relations

The marketing world is positioning itself on these two elements and advertising agencies should understand how to develop relationships with consumers for the benefit of their clients, and of course, should incorporate performance-based thinking. These can be implemented with simple technologies and a new and measurable work concept.

An advertising agency that wishes to become a significant dependable factor for its customers, should address the following five crucial issues:

1. **Advertising – primarily programmatic** – including media, assessment and data- driven marketing technologies. These are not creative solutions but rather advertising and analysis technologies.

2. **Content based marketing** – including content creation, content aggregation engines, content distribution software and, of course, analytics, measurement and optimization.
3. **Social marketing** – content creation and community activity for the brand – including distribution across all networks relevant to the brand / customer, performance measurement, automated activity management through smart software solutions.
4. **Marketology** – combining basic technologies in marketing. The world of marketing is undergoing automation of all its components. Technological tools must be part of the new culture of advertising agencies.
5. **Management and establishment of customers' digital assets** – site, stores, applications, bots, blogs, social, brand sites, brand channels on media and smart television, YouTube channels and the like. This part includes developing technologies, analytics and promotion. Keep in mind – the goal should always be to control the processes and especially data.

> An advertising agency planning to embark on this essential change will also have to change its whole recruitment strategy – more technology, data, analytics, and content people. The four anchors of change and no less important – the four main components that could bridge the knowledge gaps between an advertising agency and its clients.
>
> **"And what about creative?" you're probably asking yourself**
>
> This factor will not necessarily be part of the future advertising agency. Advertising agencies will not always keep their own traditional creative department, they will outsource specialized agencies – where you will meet a different type of worker, as well as different business models (payment per talent, payment per project, retainer, etc.).

Advertising agencies looking to continue to provide value to customers and, as we have said, also create dependency of a sort, will need to focus on the five pillars listed here and release the creative field to specialized supporters.

Chapter Twenty

The principles of brand building in the digital age

Digital platforms and technologies, as well as cultural changes and media consumption habits characterizing the digital natives, have influenced the way in which a brand can be built and maintained in this new environment. The way to build, maintain, and improve a brand goes through a number of stages and guidelines:

Think publicity & social first – then advertising

The link between a brand and its potential customers should be initially based on engagement and value. Customers' initial listening to your message will be generated through proper presence on social. Presence. Not campaigns. A brand should strive to produce an ongoing dialog with its customers which usually takes place online and through content.

Different is better than better

Do not try to do better than others. Focus on creative thinking in order to be different. The digital consumer has a rather limited degree of attention and patience; therefore, differentiation of your brand should be clear and absolute.

Distinction at the product and features level will do a great job for you. If you have not been able to offer a different product, focus on creating differentiation at the level of packaging, marketing or distribution level.

Owning a word or words

Branding in the digital world involves owning a domain, category, or even a term relevant to the target audience.

Credentials / Authenticity

Authenticity is a necessary condition for emotional bonding between consumers and the brand.

Be a Leader

Productive and market creativity may drive you to be leader in your category. Mobility supports the desired differentiation as well as creates customers' expectations. Better to be a leader – even in a relatively limited category ("the leading Japanese beer", for example).

Try to create a category

The top and most desirable edge in leading is the moment when you create a new category. Even if it initially looks like a niche category. For example, Domino's Pizza launched a delivery category long before anyone thought there was a demand or a market for it. The idea is to launch a modest initiative and gradually develop it into a more significant category. Digital platforms enable us to address the issue with a very small micro-segment and from there to build a significant category.

Brand Name

Should I choose a brand name that describes my service or product, or a creative and cool brand name? Should the brand name convey its category? You should invest creative resources at this stage. A brand name is important in establishing the identity with which the brand will run throughout its life.

On the other hand – contrary to what we were used to in the old offline era – there is no need to invest in creative slogans, because in the digital age, a brand is built through the value it provides to its customers and not by an empty yell / promise. (Does anybody remember Facebook's slogan? Or Google's?)

Singularity/ One of its kind to a unique micro-cluster

As early as in its initiation phase, the brand needs to think about the precise target audience to which it will direct its marketing resources. Our recommendation is to think of a segment called – The Passionates.
The people who are passionate about your

category are those who will try new products, adopt products, talk about them, read your content, and share it with their online friends. This should be your user profile when you are building your brand.

Distribute an idea, not just a product

The digital age requires you to spread an idea, not just a product. Digital marketing is based on relationships, not on a one-way communication. In order to strengthen this method, you should base your dialog with the consumer on something that can in time be linked to you.

Talk to people who listen to you

The fiercest marketing competition is on the attention level of the customer. He is exposed to loads of content, ideas, products and offers. It's hard to raise your brand above the noise; therefore, it is necessary to dedicate resources to locating an audience that will really listen to you, even if it is relatively small. Size does not really matter when your goal is for your captive audience to later grow and spread the word to their friends.

Use the added value of digital

The digital world has brought in its wake additional values that can be relevant to building a brand, which we have not encountered in the old traditional age. Terms such as SPOQ – Social Proof of Quality, users' involvement, engagement, sharing, exposure cycles, social buying, etc. can be very effective in establishing a successful brand. Take advantage of these promotions for your brand.

Globalism

As you build the brand, think about the world, not just about the local market where you plan to launch your product.

Brand Visualization

One of the characteristics of the native digital generation – the Y and Z generations born to digital – is visual thinking and communication. The new digital aesthetics is based on visualization. Your brand should also think visually and interact with the world accordingly.

Case Study

Building the ISIS brand through implementation of a cross-platform digital strategy

The terrorist organization based its media communication on high-quality videos, advanced graphics, polished magazines and attractive posts for a target audience characterized by its spiritual / mental state. This terrorist brand building and maintenance is based on most of the accepted guidelines in this area:

1. Visualization, iconization, intimidation, recollection.
2. Iconization – Message visualization icons have direct access to our instincts.
3. Social Familiarity / Relations
   In a place where excitement, emotional motivation, and involvement abound, ideology often begins with integration in conversation.
4. Local and global presenters.
5. **Recruitment** of the Y and Z generations – the organization combines a lot of documentation with a soft, humane and emotional message – people sitting together having pizza, watching TV together or playing on PlayStation. Content and pictures on social media, describing the pleasures of life in the caliphate, the Islamic education it provides to its citizens, and the sense of community within Islamic law.
6. **Micro-segmentation** – a cross-sectional appeal to various sub-populations, such as women, immigrants, children, youth and those who want to convert. The organization implemented micro-segmented activities, messages and packages – for

example, a micro-segment of French women, age 20-30, with anti-Western perceptions, strengthening suburban residents.
The campaign was launched with a series of interviews with Hayat Bombadein (the widow of the terrorist who carried out the attack in the kosher supermarket in Paris). These videos were distributed on YouTube and other social networks.

7. **Cross-platform media strategy**
YouTube, Viber, Facebook, Instagram, Twitter, Vimeo, Vine etc. Organization's content was spread all over the net.
8. **FOC / FOF**
Spreading fear – ISIS' most famous creation is "A Message to America", a high-quality video that shows the decapitation of American journalist James Foley. The video was distributed by running a viral campaign, using a methodology of contacts of friends of friends with distribution across all social networks.
9. **First in the category**
A promise to the "consumer" – a large global state
An Islamic super-state that combines religious, political and military rule

according to the model established by the Prophet Muhammad at the beginning of Islam. Rebranding and a greater promise: on June 29, 2014, the organization declared the establishment of the caliphate and changed its name from the Islamic State of Iraq and al-Sham to the Islamic State.

10. **Branded promoters / branded influencers**

    Branding the distributors "Knights of the Media" – Gatekeeper brands that spread the message to a loyal audience.
11. **Building an organized digital organization**
    Including official propaganda headquarters – "Al-Hayat", Rumiyah media, and Al-Furkan Media Production Agency.
12. **Distributing franchises** – the media and production organization has 20 branches. Local media offices distribute some of Al Hayat's material, as well as their own materials. For example, Dar al-Islam, a French propaganda magazine. Through the franchising system the central headquarters provides the branches with methodology, standards and propaganda material.

13. **Involvement – Forums**

Entering sites such as ASK.FM Discussions, questions and talks in forums on various sites with potential recruits. The talks are based, among others, on the reasons for their joining, how life is perceived under the organization's regime and how one can join.

Campaign Goals

Recruitment, terror / intimidation, empathy, branding, calling for Westerners to adopt Hijra (immigration to the Islamic state), call for jihad.

<u>The main principles of digital strategy / brand building of ISIS</u>

Visualization
Micro-clusters
Micro-publishers/Influencers
Focusing on generations Y & Z
Tracking the Passionate segment
Differentiation
Converting people to promoters
Short brand name
Owning a word
Publicity & Social first
Authenticity
Creating a new category

Brand values: Inspiring & Evoking Pride & Impacting Society

Chapter Twenty-one

Interaction & Engagement – Instead of – Reach & Frequency

Here are a few facts we've collected from media research done in the past year:
The number of TV viewing hours of the younger generation has cut down by almost half over the past five years. The Z generation watches television on average less than an hour a day. On YouTube, however, they spend more than two hours a day. More than 50% of US households are subscribed to Netflix. 69% consider the traditional ad format as a distraction.
When it comes to promoting a product or service, 63% prefer to listen to "real people on the net" (Influencers).

Evidently, digital consumers are looking to have a certain degree of involvement and contact with brands on social. Digital users expect a relationship based on authorization where the consumer gives the brand permission to engage in a marketing dialog. Such permission can be granted by actions such as downloading the brand's App, registering to its blog and the company's website or tracking the company's social.

Reach & Frequency – these two terms have been leading the industry for many years. Its main goal was clear and decisive – to spread our message to a maximum number of people and preferably expose each of them as many times as possible to what the brand has to say about itself. These terms are no longer relevant. Today, the only way to initiate successful marketing moves is to adopt different words.

Interaction & Engagement

A targeted approach should be embraced for micro-segments. Ask their permission to market, create a relationship with them and provide them with value. That's how correct marketing should be done. Size does not matter; digital knowhow is the way to go, especially for smaller brands that try to bridge gaps with the big ones.

Chapter Twenty-two

The end of the advertising agency as we know it

The advertising industry in the United States feels uncomfortable with the strengthening of the so-called In-House Marketing trend. More and more super-brands are moving towards owning their programmatic advertising – L'Oréal, Netflix, Unilever, Walmart, Target, with strong brands looking for the right structure to ensure their dominance.

Super brands understand that they need to control the data of their marketing-related activity – customer media consumption habits, campaign performance, campaign responses, campaign-purchase correlation, user profile information and usage. All these are valuable treasures for brands and companies. The decision to "bring home" this treasure is adopted more and more by brands in the programmatic era.

In other words, programmatic advertising (which makes up the big share of brands' advertising activity) is gradually leaving the conventional advertising agencies behind. Add to that the fact that brands manage campaigns on Facebook and Google quite well by themselves, and you end up with a gloomy picture of the advertising agencies, as we have known them not long ago.

How can advertising agencies deal with the situation?
The solution lies in advertising agencies adopting technologies so that they can provide a technological answer to all those brands that are unable to buy / manufacture their own programmatic advertising. Agencies should move towards this goal, focus less on mega-brands, preferring to tackle different ones (most of the market). The movement of brands is usually slow. You can take advantage of the momentum, with one condition: **implementing a start-up mentality in advertising agencies**. First of all, creating media opportunities that are not based on Facebook or Google, where advertising agencies have no leverage, moving towards a significant entry into content.

Inbound Marketing – developing skills in content creation and content distribution
Brands should start thinking like creatives. Those who can help them cross this road are the new advertisers / creative people.

It is time for advertising agencies to spearhead this industry
In short, bridging the technological gap between the advertising agency and its customers is a necessary condition. Developing expertise in non-conventional creative areas (content – including smart

content distribution capabilities) is no less important.

Without these two basic changes, the industry will lose the relevance required for its continued existence.

Chapter Twenty-three

Is great creative less important than ever?

With the development of smart targeting technologies, the table returns to a discussion that has kept quite a few people in the advertising industry on their toes: what is the specific role of creativity in marketing processes? How much brands should allocate to it, as opposed to targeting and moving consumers to venues, which could most likely generate successful business.

Imagine the following scenario:
A brand – a retail chain, for example – defines its relevant audience as a 40-year-old male who lives in the north part of the city and experiences hair loss. He is extremely interested in natural beauty products and has purchased hair products last year for a total of $1,000. It is also evident that this man downloaded that retail chain's app and pops into digital natural products stores once a week.
The retail chain holds this person's social profile and knows his needs and purchasing habits. So, all this retailer needs to do is send him an offer to buy a relevant product – now. Perhaps coupled with an attractive incentive.
What's going on here?

Relevance – check
Intention to Buy – check
Purchasing Power – check
Category Passion – check
A perceived need – check

There is no need for creativity and fireworks
Just reach the right person, at the right time, with the right information and product.
Some would say this is an extreme segmentation / information / reaching scenario.

Maybe, but we are not far away from this stage; platforms such as Facebook and Google are already monitoring us to the very end. And what's more, social networks such as Facebook invite us to produce highly segmented campaigns using their dashboard without any need for professional creative. **Facebook is, in my opinion, the most significant standard-bearer of the approach that minimizes the weight of traditional creative in the marketing process.**

Social networks rely on small-medium businesses as its growth engine. It invites them to create a streamlined, efficient and simple advertising activity without the need to hire creative people or an advertising agency. In the not too distant future, targeting and reaching the individual customer level will be the norm.

Chapter Twenty-four

The Comeback of Testimonials

Testimonials – the personal testimony of users and customers – is a creative format that has seen good days in the history of advertising. People who have experienced a particular product or service, talking to people who have not yet tried it, is considered an advertising format that has worked well for a very long time in certain categories. Over time, questions were raised about the effectiveness of this advertising tool, especially regarding its reliability.

The big question is whether customers tend to believe that the person issuing all these recommendations actually exists. And if so, will their attachment increase? What makes the message more or less reliable? Is there a need for high production quality or perhaps an authentic production will have a better impact? After years during which this format enjoyed massive popularity, its efficiency began to drop as consumers started to question its reliability. Consequently, the term testimonials underwent re-visualization in the digital-social era and took on a new natural and organic configuration almost free of the involvement of advertisers and creative people. It is called:

PURE – Post-Usage Reviews

It is the term that drives the ever-increasing category of the marketing industry.

It is part of the rising category of SPOQ – Social Proof of Quality, a super-term that describes all the channels through which people influence others in their purchasing decisions and preference of a product or service. People tell their online neighbors about products they have bought or services they have used and thus influence their buying decisions, more than any other planned marketing move. The following are a few configurations of this organic-marketing-organic format, in which brands can integrate and influence:

1. PURE – Post-Usage Reviews – quotes from real customers. We all tend to share so a brand can use this tendency by opening sharing areas that look authentic and reliable.
2. Social Posts – social networks are the most natural place for customers to share their experiences, so brands can "recruit" real posts as brand promoters. Brand measurement engines enable you to identify how customers relate to your brand, and then you can use some of them as reliable and effective marketing vehicles.

3. Video Testimonials – production quality is not considered an important factor when it comes to authentic and real testimonials. This fact, combined with the fact that YouTube video distribution channels are open and user friendly, makes it an easy-to-use, organic video-based impact channel for any brand or business. In addition, it is important to remember that video is the most widely shared format – more than text or image. That is why testimonial videos are perhaps the best marketing product to influence the buying habits of potential customers.

4. Interviews – well-organized interviews with clients and / or experts and / or opinion leaders is the more structured and perhaps less authentic form of testimonials. Yet, in the right quantity, it has merit and should be included in your platform.

Chapter Twenty-five

Customer Centrality Formula –The ultimate organic advertising format

Placing the consumer at the center of the organization's marketing and business strategy has been the conceptual or practical goal of different brands and companies for years. Yet only now in the digital age can it really be done and measured correctly and effectively.

How do you do it?
Listen – by using SPOQ – Social Proof of Quality tools and social sentiment mining. First you need to understand what customers and consumers think about your brand, the company's products and the quality of service they are getting. Digital platforms, sites and apps allow us to listen to people who are the most important to our business. Listening technologies are accessible to every company or business and produce reliable reports on your brand status.

PURE – Post-Usage Reviews – this marketing activity is turning out to be the most effective tool in your work plans. The impact of consumer experiences is much more significant than any advertising or promotional message you use today. You should definitely prepare for this conceptual change.

Create – user's profile and micro-clusters. The next step is to create clusters of target audiences not based only on the interests and needs of customers but also on how closely they are to your brand, or in other words, where they stand in terms of their feelings towards your company. A user listening tool allows you to draw a map of customer proximity to your brand.

Deliver – customized value. Based on the characteristics of your target audience, including their position on the sentiment curve, you should create a value-added offer for your potential customers coupled with content-based values.

A brand that successfully implements these three anchors will be able to pick the fruits of success that differentiate it from its competitors:
- **Recognition** – as in understanding the value that a brand brings to a customer. In crowded markets, this is a differentiating factor that can serve as basis for a consumer-brand relationship.
- **Loyalty** – the recognition that has been created could open the gate to customer

loyalty that can in turn lead to a successful sales dialog.

- Convert users to brand promoters

The highest quality level in digital marketing moves is the one that converts customers into brand promoters. There consumers share their positive experience by interacting with the brand and promoting its interests, all in a natural and organic manner based on recognition of the value of the brand and its products.

Chapter Twenty-six

Traditional Advertising will play a minor role in the marketing mix

The traditional **One-To-Many advertising** format where one source (advertiser / brand) tries to convince consumers (on TV, magazines and sites) to buy or choose its product and/ or service is well known. Yet it is gradually losing its power and impact and is going to play only a limited role in the marketing value chain in the coming years. Three main components are about to replace it, which will lead the marketing dialog between companies and potential consumers / customers:

1. **SPOQ – Social Proof of Quality**
   People's reviews influence our decisions much more than any creative advertisement. The **SPOQ Index** is based on sentiment and volume, which we all use when choosing a hotel, for example, on sites such as Booking and Expedia. The travel industry is leading the usage of SPOQ as a prime tool to help us in our purchase decisions. Leisure brands should invest in improving their

SPOQ Index instead of launching a new expensive TV campaign. This trend will take over all other categories and will change the relations between companies and people. How can companies improve their SPOQ Index?

- Set genuine relationship with users and customers. An in-depth relationship ensures users are happy to share their (good) experience about your products and services.
- Brands should create friendly recommendations areas on their sites and apps.
- Brands should ask users to share their experience and consider some personal reward for their contribution.
- Loyalty programs can work very well in improving brands' SPOQ Index.
- Brands should keep a fruitful dialog with customers on their site. That will encourage users to write and share.
- Brands should include users' comments and recommendations as a main factor in their campaign.

2. UIA – User Initiated Advertisement

Improved search-based ads and offerings will still be significant in the years to come. Google and Amazon will lead this category, but we will meet new segmented players that will play a significant role in reaching their micro-segmented target audience.

3. Content Marketing

Brands should think like publishers and invest resources in creating unique content and utilities that will enable them to build long lasting relations with their target audience. Bringing value to users and potential consumers is a key factor in brands' marketing success. Brands should understand how to build the right content mix and become experts in Content Distribution – including in Programmatic Content Distribution.

The **SPOQ/UIA/Content** triangle is about to be the anchor of brands' Go-To-Market Plan and requires deep changes in companies' marketing strategy.

Chapter Twenty-seven

Mobile Marketing

Reach your ideal customers via their personal device

Ten steps in launching a Mobile application. From concept to Go-To-Market.

In order to secure a dialog with enough people on ample relevant meeting points it is necessary to have a presence of a cross-platform brand. When it comes to young audiences, the most significant step is to interact with them through their smartphone. These modern devices are actually small powerful computers that enable their users to do almost anything while on the move – shopping, watching videos, social, and of course, business. This device is currently their most personal one on which they have become dependent and somehow addicted to, which necessitates directing the digital presence of brands and businesses to it.

A business or a company who decides to include Mobile Marketing in its ongoing strategy has to go through several stages, from concept to success:

1. **Determining users' needs** – the company marketing or content people should initially define the need they plan to meet with their application. For example, answering a basic need, promoting a better life for a specific audience, saving money or time, fun, community interactions, social contact, upgrading information, or pushing for personal empowerment. A brand can decide to generate an app that meets more than one need.
2. **Target audience definition** – one of the most important stages. It looks to define the audience which the app intends to target. This is more than defining socioeconomic characteristics. It needs to do more. Come up with data which will enable us to build an effective profile of our customers – who they are, who their friends are, what their interests are, which groups they have joined on social, whom they influence, and by whom are they influenced, their digital habits, their digital shopping, and the like.
3. **Benefits** – a list of benefits for consumers with whom we wish to build a relationship.
4. **Roadmap** – designing the application features and the roadmap for the coming year.

5. **Competitive environment** – draw up a competition table consisting of three competitors and five features, comparing what we are about to provide in our app to that of our competitors. Based on the comparison table we will develop a USP – a Unique Selling Proposition for our app launching.
6. **Goals** – we should set our quantitative and qualitative goals: For example, the number of downloads for the first year of activity, daily / weekly / monthly users, user usage data, bounce rate retention data, removal data, Engagement Index based on SPOQ Index (how many comments you get on App stores), user-based typology and the way content is consumed in the app.
7. **Business models** – some brands use a platform just to strengthen or promote their products. They combine a business model that generates new revenue for the company. A business model can be based on:
    - Advertising
    - Transactions
    - Subscriptions
    - Freemium (free use combined with paid upgrades)
    - License fee

8. **GTM** – Go-To-Market plan. One should set a precise and detailed plan for launching and ongoing marketing.

   The first step will be to promote traffic to the app store and encourage followers to download the brand app. Downloads start with creating awareness – by using advertising, PR, social, and content-based marketing. Combining all of them will set up the plan of how to reach the market.

   The next step will focus on user retention. This is primarily done through bringing real value to users that includes content, creating triggers for app return, and endless distribution and sharing. Next step will be to take care of users' usage. Frequency is a key parameter. A good MAU/DAU ratio (the ratio between Monthly Active Users and Daily Active Users) usually ensures a successful business.

9. **Budget** – any brand or company mobile activity is usually part of the company's overall development and marketing budget. A development budget has to be defined to include content maintenance, manpower,

infrastructure and technology, social promotion, promotion through mobile campaigns, collaborations with other relevant applications, public relations, marketing activity through Influencers and, if necessary, support from offline media.

It is very important to manage all operations with application management, measurement and analytics platforms such as: www.appannie.com

Chapter Twenty-eight

Mobile application promotion

The three layers of activity necessary for success

Google's and Apple's app stores are carrying millions of apps and the market continues to grow. As the capabilities of mobile devices improve, more and more technologies find their way to app configuration. Competition has become fierce, the market is crowded and borderless – that is, apps no longer have to compete with just a limited number of local competitors. Local application manufacturers and distributors are facing competition from millions of apps on Apple's and Google's stores.

And that's not all – if you've been able to convince potential users to **download your app** to their mobile device, bear in mind that the most difficult part is getting them to **stay with you.** 26% of those who downloaded your app will open it once and never come back. Potential customers will give you one single chance to convince them that your app brings them real value. That means, as we have said here about digital marketing in general, you need to know your customers, their needs, their desires and what triggers will work for them – which should happen as early as the development phase of the application!!!!! Only then can you continue to define the exact segment (micro-clustering) and tackle the activity of promoting the application to them.

An equally important move is, of course, the need to convince your potential customers to make real **use** of the app at a reasonable frequency that will justify the whole thing, in terms of both business and marketing.
If you succeed in the three essential steps of persuading enough people to download and use your app, your reward could be significant – being part of the daily life of your potential user / consumer.

But, as you can see, the road is long. After all, remember that the average American downloads an average of 80 apps throughout his device's lifetime (a little more than two years) but uses only 13 – including basic ones such as email, weather, social, etc. In other words, the empty space on the shelf is quite limited.
The way to promote your app goes through three solutions: organic promotion, media promotion, and content promotion.

How do I promote my store's app?

Organic promotion (SEO)

1. Begin with a written brief containing the following lists:

A list of the app's function – which primary category does the app belong to, and which subcategory.

2. Choose key words – track the words that are relevant to the category. This is done by studying the competitors and using a database of companies that specialize in creating such lists.
3. What to do with these key words? Best to combine 3-5 key words in the title, as well as in the first paragraph of the product description on the store. The list of relevant words should be updated and refreshed once every two weeks. Do not forget to include a list of detailed app's features as well as links to all of the brand's digital assets – site, social, etc.

Media Promotion
One click installation.
This is the term that should guide you through all your activities on the relevant media – including brand own media (branches, social sites etc.)

Content Promotion
Guerrilla activity in relevant networks and forums.

- Collaborate with relevant bloggers. From our experience, it is best to work with small and focused bloggers – they do a better (and cheaper) job for brands and app owners.
- Testimonials – real users' experiences do a great job for app owners.
- The next step – after we've convinced enough people to download our app and use it, our first goal is to convince them to return and become regular users.

How do we get the user to come back and share our app with their friends and do the promoting work for us?

- The most important thing is to produce relevant, up-to-date, engaging content and turn users to our brand promoters, sharing it with their friends.
- Unique content and unique value (or one that looks like it) for a specific group will generate an incentive with the group members to share with their friends.
- Gamification – turning some of your content into a competitive game does a great job in creating a trigger for sharing, especially if the game has a competitors' table. There is no need for prizes but there is a need for a sense of advancement and victory.

Chapter Twenty-nine

Near Field Marketing

A necessary supplement for brands that are looking to market to young people

Most brands invest a substantial amount of resources at the starting point of the marketing chain – creating awareness, persuasion, brand preference, creating an incentive for shopping, and so on.

Yet only a few brands, even digital ones, invest in their last mile – a smart promotion digital activity at the point of sale.

Most of the activities in this important area are channeled to our smartphone, led by the Z generation. Born in the mid-90s, they lead the mobile shopping category.
43% of young people use mobiles in the store or mall to compare prices.
42% of young buyers use mobiles to consult friends or family about the purchase itself.
35% use the mobile to search for current sales opportunities.

The time when the potential customer uses his mobile to learn more about products / prices / alternatives and at the same time consults with his friends and family about his planned purchase – is considered **the walled garden**.

Ostensibly, brands and companies do not have a foothold or influence on this process. However, in the digital age, brands can do something to influence potential consumers. Research clearly shows that brands that have succeeded in creating a valuable ongoing **relationship** with this segment are given preference when making purchasing decisions, even during these "field" activities.

Location-based activity is the ultimate brand solution for the "walled garden" phenomenon. The NFM – Near Field Communication, an effective way to do that, is by launching branded chatbots on location-based platforms such as SnapTech or Facebook and / or persuading the client to download the brand's mobile app.

Then the brand will be able to "accompany" the potential customer in his or her deliberations in the store or mall. Basic opportunity-oriented products such as personal digital coupons based on an in-depth familiarity with the customer's needs – will do a great job. The "Last Mile" activity is a significant cornerstone in completing a market-familiar move when it comes to the Z generation. Remember, this is a segment that is no longer very accessible through traditional screens – TV, portals, etc.

Chapter Thirty

Mobile Marketing

Three anchor activities that should fit into your marketing plan

Our smartphones have long stood as a clear target for anyone engaged in marketing and branding. What makes Mobile Marketing necessary and strategic for companies, businesses and brands?

- These small devices are powerful computers and enable us to use them for almost anything we need.
- It is our personal device, and somewhat intimate, even for a marketing dialog.
- The small screen, touching distance away, ensures better attention than any other digital device.

There are three anchor activities that you should integrate into your work plan.

1. **User-Persuasive Vehicles**

Mobile by nature is the only device we keep with us all the time (almost). This allows the brand to create a consumer dialog by supplying value, which should end in moving the consumer from a non-business relationship venue to one with a potential to develop a business dialog. For example, personal coupons based on in-depth acquaintance with the consumer are an excellent transportation tool or Persuasive Vehicles that enable the brand to create a measurable trigger for sales activity, including follow-up.

2. Location-based promotion

Mobile is the only device that enables reaching the consumer in his actual location. This is a marketing initiative based on the relevance of Here & Now. Proper use of the location of the target audience will transform it from a potential client to an actual consumer.

For example, a retail chain that locates the potential customer in the vicinity of its branch and invites him to step in and enjoy a unique and special personal offering increases its chances of success based on a relevant location point.

3. Advertising and marketing based on behavioral data

This small, efficient device stays with us all the time, through which we perform activities of all kinds: shopping, information, comparing prices, locating stores, locating opportunities, social interaction and so on. This means that if we were able to

persuade potential customers to download the brand app or connect to our ChatBot, it will provide us with a consumer database based on user multi-layered behavior.
Not just data based on interests or social behavior, but one that relates to the real, everyday behavior of us all. Based on such an extensive dataset, the brand can design its product strategy, its marketing strategy and the type and manner in which it operates, including its creativity.

Chapter Thirty-one

Mobile marketing fully automates all layers of activity

Marketing, media and content are being automated. More and more technological solutions are changing the industry and turning advertising, public relations, product development and content, easier, cheaper, accessible to companies and businesses, and consequently affect the organizational and functional structure of organizations of all kinds:

1. Content creation

Content-based marketing has become a strategic and necessary component in the activity of brands and companies of all kinds. The most effective content format which gets the biggest amount of sharing is video. The need to create video content on a daily basis is ripe ground for the development of technologies that allow the brand to produce clips automatically. All you need to do is fill the "machine" with texts, music clips and pictures and within seconds you get a video clip that describes your product or any other topic you wish to promote.

An effective solution in this field was invented by Magisto: https://www.magisto.com

More and more companies maintain a professional or experiential blog as part of their digital presence spider. Writing a blog is not a simple task and requires an almost daily creative commitment. There are technological solutions that automatically generate text based on the subject matter required for writing articles for the company blog. The existing solutions are not perfect yet, but some are definitely in the right direction. One example is Articoolo: http://articoolo.com/

2. Automatic PR

Ongoing work with a conventional PR agency can be expensive for most companies. Automated platforms allow low-budget companies to distribute messages through targeted public relations campaigns. These solutions invite companies to write a communiqué and choose a basic (territory, language) target audience. These platforms will automatically distribute the marketing message to thousands of sites. Prices can range from $100 to $300 per campaign. These platforms support public relations needs of companies and businesses that cannot invest tens of thousands of dollars in public relations. Examples of such solutions are:

www.prweb.com

www.marketwired.com

3. Managing brand activity on social networks

Brands and companies have acknowledged the need to establish presence on social networks. The process is simple and includes being present on several social networks as well as on digital assets at the same time. Managing all these has become complex in light of the new existing alternatives – writing the right content, distributing it at the right time on the relevant social networks, measuring the performance of each post on all platforms, and optimizing all that on the go. All these are managed today automatically and efficiently by dedicated companies such as:

hootsuite, marketo

hubspot.

4. Mobile application management and tracking

One of the most important tools in mobile is Appannie. It provides the application owner with performance data automatically – who downloaded, who deleted, how many showed interest, how many left, usage data, user profile, application status compared to competitors, relevant trends in the category and so on. Everything is automatic, user-friendly and up to date: www.appannie.com

5. Automatic development of mobile applications

In bygone times development used to bite a significant portion of the budget of companies or businesses. Today development is simple, easy and cheap, consequently shifting most of the energy and resources to the marketing and customer retention phase. Many solutions offer creative possibilities for automatic development of mobile applications.

www.bobile.com

www.appsvillage.com

6. Setting up an E-shop

E-commerce – mobile and other platforms – has turned fully automated. Today there is no need to invest significant resources in the establishment and operation of an online store. If you have a product to sell and you have the marketing knowhow of a digital store, you can get all your operational support from companies like Shopify.

www.shopify.com

7. Programmatic advertising

The Advertising Industry is the most affected by automation. Programmatic advertising on mobile as well as on desktop is tailored to the real-time destination, namely, where to display the ad in real-time bidding (RTB). The ad presented to the user is based on his personal information and the price that the advertisers are prepared to pay. All that is done automatically with no human footprint of salespeople or a dialog between the supply side (sites and applications) and the demand side (brands, advertising agencies, etc.). Today, more than 80% of the digital advertising budgets in the United States are used programmatically. This domain, like other advertising ones, is dominated by Google and Facebook with potential competition from Amazon.

How will the automation trend affect the industry?

- Functional change – some traditional professions will disappear.
- Opportunity for small companies to bridge budget-dependent gaps when competing with large and rich companies.
- Marketing and customer retention will become more important (compared to development and product).

Chapter Thirty-two

MFS – Mobile First Strategy

Is this strategy good for you?

Mobile has become our main screen. The question is how to use this personal medium to produce effective marketing, taking into account that it is not necessarily suitable for every company in the same way.

The market should be divided into three main categories.

1. Mobile First Category

This category consists of companies and products which find it worthwhile to implement a mobile-targeted marketing strategy. Defining companies which fit this category includes three components:

Brands that exist in our physical space and / or are characterized by low involvement and / or belong to the category of impulsive purchasing.

- Brands that exist in the physical space belong to categories such as convenience stores, fuel companies, retailers in various fields (food, fashion, pharma, electrical appliances, household products, toiletries, etc.), transportation services (taxis), leisure and recreation (restaurants, concerts, etc.).

- A low involvement product, one where purchasing it does not involve major decision-making or a thorough market research on the part of the consumer. Low involvement products include food, convenience store, fuel, retail, transportation, leisure and entertainment.
- The list of categories of impulse buying includes companies such as fashion, footwear, food, leisure and culture.

The more a brand fits into more items of this triangular formula (physical space, low involvement, impulsive buying) it should implement a more radical strategy of:

Mobile First Strategy

Focusing on mobile marketing, which includes dedicated micro-segmental applications that include content, community, developing – bots for continuous contact with customers, launch of COP – Commercial Opportunity Products (such as coupons or the brand's digital currency) and, of course, relevant and original content that should create a long-term relationship between the brand and its mobile customers.

Members of this category can gradually relinquish any investments in other media such as radio, television and billboards, and focus on Mobile & Social as prime elements of the Go-To-Market plan

What role does mobile play in this category?

- Sales channel – creating a measurable and accurate revenue source – marketing channel – generates brand preference

What do you measure in this category?

Traffic to the physical or digital store, sales, purchase frequency, purchase volume per visit, frequency of visits, revenue, profitability, distribution of purchases by products and categories, price sensitivity by product and triggers (which offers and COP [Commercial Opportunity Products] such as coupons work better).

2. Mobile Marketing Category

Companies belonging to this category will have one component of the triangular formula (physical space, low involvement, impulsive buying).

These companies should prepare for mobile marketing but not focus solely on mobile activity as part of their marketing strategy. In other words, it makes sense to launch a mobile application and invest in promoting it while examining the ROMI – Return on Marketing Investment

What is the role of mobile in this category?

Here too, mobile platform enables differentiation and preference, as well as the creation of a relationship and increased interaction between consumers and brand, and brand assets.

What do you measure in this category?

- Users' Engagement

- SPOQ – Social Proof of Quality Index

  In other words, to what extent does our mobile activity succeed in getting users to respond to our marketing activity, and become brand promoters – users who write, respond, and recommend?

- Depth and quality of the brand-user relationship (brand preference indicator).

- Influence on purchase volume and frequency.

3. Mobile Presence Category
Companies belonging to this category do not meet any of the formula components:

Mobile First Strategy formula: Psychical Presence & Low Engagement Products & Impulsive Buying Products.

Companies in this category should not ignore the fact that the mobile device is our most significant device and therefore must create a mobile presence – mobile site, forming mobile campaigns etc.

However, companies of this type will not find real marketing value by launching and promoting applications, which will come at the expense of other marketing activities.

Keep in mind that developing a mobile application is the first and easiest step. The significant and Sisyphean stage is a running ongoing marketing plan which reaches significant, relevant audiences, persuades them to download your app and, of course, continuous work on maintaining significant usage performance and retention.

These are huge marketing investments mainly suitable for companies and brands of the first category (Mobile First) and a few in the second category (Mobile Marketing).

Companies in the third category can give up huge investments in the complex field of mobile-based application marketing.

What is the role of mobile in this company category?

Cross-platform presence creates an opportunity for more contact between brands and consumers.

What do you measure in the third category?

Analyze usage of platform distribution (site, mobile, social) including the type of content consumed on each platform.

The depth of mobile marketing activity varies from company to company and from category to category according to the suitability to the components of the formula:

Psychical Presence & Low Engagement Products & Impulsive Buying Products

Chapter Thirty-three

The Future of Publishers and Media Companies

Six characteristics that are about to lead the media and content industry in the coming years

Evidently, the technological developments we have been witnessing in recent years bear a significant impact on the way we consume media and content. The relationship that characterizes the triangle – content producers-brands-consumers – has undergone significant changes, consequently positioning consumers at the center. The power has clearly shifted to them. They have more choice, more control, and more alternatives.

These developments are about to change the media industry and re-evaluate it on the basis of six key anchors:

Publishers:

DDP –Detachable Digital Publishers

Generations Y and Z get their information and content while surfing on social networks. Noticing the depleting traffic from this important segment publishers are beginning to implement a strategy of **Detachable Digital Publishers** – DDP, creating small content pieces and distributing it on social media channels and messaging platforms like Snap or Viber. This is the new breed of media companies. They cannot lure young users to their content, so they bring their content to them.

CNN, NBC and Hearst Media Super brands have launched dedicated content channels for Snap users. The new format will transform media companies into content ones and deepen their expertise in content distribution and monetization solutions away from home.

Content nature:

Snackable Content & Visualization

Content in the digital age becomes short, adapted to a young target audience. The term Snackable Content is about to flood digital industry adapting it to a target audience of a short attention span and for the one leading platform – the smartphone. Content producers need to consider the fact that all content must meet the three Aces: the requirement that all content must be **Snackable-Shareable-Searchable**.

Content producers need to think about the suitability of the content to the requirements of search engines, building the content in a way that will allow easy distribution and sharing in a compressed, simple and chewed form.

Brands think like publishers

Brands understand that they cannot conduct effective marketing without building a relationship with potential customers and consumers, which is impossible to create without bringing them value. It means a strategic entry into the content domain. Brands wishing to make it are beginning to think like publishers. In today's market, they have one advantage over the publishers: they have resources and budgets to create, purchase and distribute content.

The traditional media industry is being shaken with the penetration of social a part of our daily lives with a significant proportion of traditional players weakening and largely disappearing. Brands that adopt a smart content strategy will be able to join in and appropriate a domain or relevant segment. For example: Redbull has become the leader in the field of extreme sports. American Express has taken ownership of content and support for small businesses. Over the next few years, brands of every kind and size will assimilate publishers' thinking as part of their marketing strategy and reshape the media and content industry.

Permission-Based Content Distribution

Content creation is the anchor for all marketing in the new era. Yet this is a complex task which basically depends on the ability of the content producer to distribute it to the right audience.

In an age of crowded messages and continuous struggle for audience attention, gaining permission is a basic condition for any move – if a consumer does not give the brand his permission to receive its message, such a move is useless. The good news for brands is that there are many junctions which they can use to get their customers' early approval – downloading a mobile app is considered approval, as well as registering a brand blog, a Facebook friendship, or a customer that follows a brand on Instagram or Twitter.

In other words, no authorization means no relationship.

On the other hand, there are many options for creating a relationship based on authorization. All that needs to be done is to produce content of value to a defined and distinct audience. Good content opens the door for users' permission.

Immersive Content (playful experience):

Virtual Reality & Augmented Reality

AR (Augmented Reality) & VR (Virtual Reality) – In the coming years these technologies will become widespread in content creation and market moves. We believe that Virtual Reality will become prevalent and effective for marketers, because it allows content and value to become accessible by adding a new layer of activity – on top of the basic layer of reality, as we perceive it.

These technologies have already reached their maturity with their strength lying in their simplicity and the value they can produce for consumers, brands and content owners. This can be expressed in applications such as on-the-go guide, information about businesses and restaurants, museums and art, product interaction and its components at point of sale or remote, multi-sensory play or applications of interactive learning.

Everything is ready for multi-layered accessibility and a richer experience of content of every kind.

Reward-based relations with users

The content area, as well as other areas, is going to be affected by Blockchain technology implementing more and more token-based micropayments options.

These applications will change the nature of the relationship between media and content companies and users.

For their contribution as content creators or content consumers, users will be rewarded with tokens following a simple set-up – the more tokens they gather the bigger their impact on the site. Their content will be promoted as well as their feedback with whoever is more active winning more tokens (you can also buy tokens).

These six key anchors of the media and content industry require Media and Content companies to prepare themselves for the new age in terms of technology, ideas and marketing. Otherwise, their future is questionable.

As was mentioned, a new type of player has joined the media industry in the past year and is about to change the way media companies contemplate their future – **DDP – Detachable Digital Publisher.**

This creature – the detachable publisher – is not trying to bring readers or users to his site. It tries to bring his content to readers / users, to the places and digital areas where they live (Snap, WhatsApp, Facebook etc.) or generate content-based interaction with potential consumers using bots that will initiate dialog through popular messaging software.

Social networks – and now messaging platforms – have changed our lives and the way we (primarily Millennials) consume content. The most significant change lies in the fact that young people get everything they need – news, fashion, information, trends, sports, and so forth, on the go through social networks. The source is no longer necessarily an official media factor but rather friends and friends of friends (FOF).

This means that young consumers are no longer using media companies' websites or apps, which in turn requires marketers to think differently and implement a completely different contact and marketing strategy.

Media companies that have previously based their business on their destination sites should think like content companies. They no longer insist on bringing users to their content, but instead introduce their users with relevant detachable content pieces on every platform they are found on.

Detachable Digital Publishers (DDP) are essential for their continued existence. Not as media companies but rather as content ones. A type of player that produces and distributes content, smartly packaged for its target audience through popular social platforms.

This is possible to initiate on any platform accessible to the relevant segment – YouTube, Facebook, Twitter, Instagram and so on, enabling the implementation of a valid business model.

Media companies that turned into content companies have uploaded channels of short content to several social networks at the same time. Each platform has specific content, a defined and characterized audience with changing business models. It's not simple, but for any media / publisher company that wishes to survive and even grow this is the only way to go.

Chapter Thirty-four

Two moves that media companies have to do to compete with Facebook and Google

Too many TV channels make a living from advertising.

Too many radio stations make a living from advertising.

Thousands of sites and applications base their business model on advertising revenue.

And the advertisement pie? It's shrinking and re-calculating its path.

This new route does not include significant budget cuts for non-smart, non-targeted, less measurable platforms. In other words, the significant new parts of the advertising pie will not turn to television channels and sites lacking customer data, generic applications and, of course, traditional newspapers.

The direction is clear – most of advertising budgets go to smart media platforms, mainly the big tribes of **Google, Facebook, and Amazon** – the most accurate players in terms of data-targeting capabilities.

The Advertising and Marketing industry needs to rethink two main issues:

1. The advertising budgets that go to media companies cannot be cut by 50% (this is the forecast for the next two years), while content costs, production and development remains more or less unchanged.

   Automation technologies need to be implemented in content and production. These solutions are available.

   In addition, it is necessary to adopt an extreme approach to micro-segmental activity in media and content. For example, some bloggers and YouTubers around the world show amazing profit and loss data. Why? Because production costs, investment in content and development remains negligible, while revenues rise at an impressive rate.

   It is time to implement the change. TV companies should (really) start thinking and acting as content companies, on any platform, for any audience.

TV players are encouraged to think a bit like YouTube – small, thin, aiming at a clear cluster of consumers and above all, function as an independent profit and loss unit. Bringing value does not necessarily entail a high budget. The formula for a successful YouTube channel lies with a passionate content creator who creates a channel for passionate content consumers (those who are passionate for the same category), who are smart, small and highly defined (micro-cluster).

Websites need to implement a bloggers' thinking and action framework – small, thin, efficient, addressing a clear micro-segment with clear value creation for advertisers who wish to work smarter on the **Micro-publisher – Micro-cluster – Micro-budget** triangular basis:

The End of Mass is Here!!!!

Targeting & Social Intelligence –

Traditional media players should implement technology platforms for targeting, user profiling and accurate measurement.

Advertisers choose to invest in Facebook and Google because they offer social intelligence data, control, simple planning and performance analytics. You will not find this on linear TV or on any traditional sites. Technological solutions such as these already exist for television, sites and for applications.

And most importantly, start getting to really know your customers, otherwise there's no chance that smart advertisers will invest in your media.

Chapter Thirty-five

Tribal wars in the media industry

The big players have their problems too.

In addition to all the geopolitical developments that are wreaking havoc with our world (North Korea, Russia, Iran, Syria and the Middle East, etc.), there is a different kind of war raging.

This is the fight for our attention, our personal information, a sophisticated battle for our free time and money.

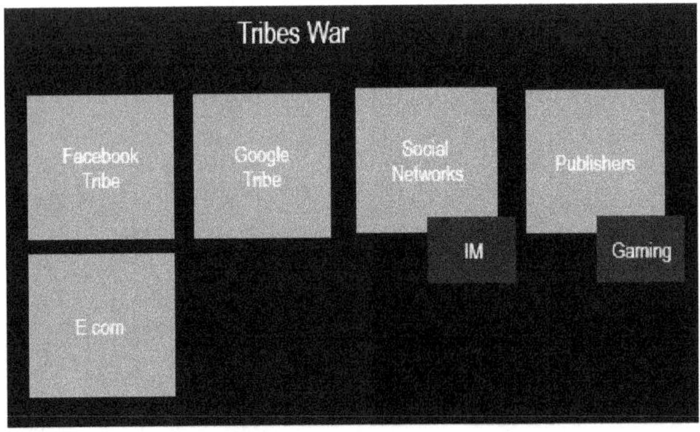

Five tribes are taking part in this ongoing struggle

1. **The Facebook tribe**

Consists of the largest social network in the world (despite signs of it weakening), Instagram acquired by the corporation in 2012 for 1 billion dollars, WhatsApp bought in 2014 for 19 billion dollars.

2. **The Google tribe**

Which includes all of the Internet's giant assets including YouTube, sharing sites, search engine and all technology companies acquired over the years.

3. **The media tribe companies**

The digital publishers who are experiencing a decline in demand and revenue since the strengthening of the two leading tribes.

The social networking tribe
There you can find players who made their debut with communication / instant messaging software and became powerful social networks with more than 100 million permanent users each.

There are many such players, some of whom control the markets or territories on which they focus and specialize. For example: Line (Japan), Wechat (China), Tango, Viber, Kakao (Japan, Korea), Telegram, Zalo (Vietnam), Kik

(Canada) and many others who are trying to become global players by detracting from Facebook.

The e-commerce players' tribe

Here, too, we are talking about a strong and powerful tribe that is reaching out to other areas such as original content, advertising products and storage services. The main and most impressive player in this tribe is, of course, Amazon.

The fierce battles between the tribes will not necessarily end with a knockout, but my bet is that **Amazon will win out in most sectors**.

The giant presents impressive revenue and profitability data, but this is not an indication of its strategic victory. The most important element of these marketing battles is **consumer dependency.**

Consumer dependency:
Amazon consumers – primarily Americans – have become dependent on the Amazon platform but not just it. It turns out that that dependence is dripping into everything that this giant brand produces – content, services, video, and so forth. In addition, Amazon knows its consumers better than its giant competitors, and recognizes our actual consumer behavior.

Unlike Google, which focuses on our interests or Facebook, which recognizes our social behavior, Amazon collects real information about our purchases, frequency, profile and scope of financial investment.

The combination of this kind of information and the dependence that Amazon has managed to produce in us, plus the real value it brings to our lives, guarantees its supremacy in the inter-tribal war.

So what about the traditional media companies?

In recent years the situation of the media companies / publishers has worsened considerably.

It got worse although it's not over for them yet

Why did it get worse?

Users are trickling to other alternatives – mainly social. There they not only meet friends but are also exposed to the news, learn about fashion, trends and gossip – they get everything as they move on social networks. This is called **The Age of Discovery** – gathering information and social intelligence, while hanging out and staying on social.

In addition, advertisers have also chosen to streamline their advertising budgets to more accurate options (Google and Facebook). Most media companies lose money and users on a monthly basis. Some publishers have given up – actively seeking mergers, cutting investments in content and implementing thin marketing programs.

Why do we think the fate of the business is yet to be decided? Most traditional media companies have unique characteristics. Users still value high quality content and if these companies are still capable of packing their content correctly and updating it, they have a chance to win the battle and survive.

The solution is based on three terms that will be very dominant in the coming year:

Detachable Publishers

This refers to a publisher behaving as a content producer rather than a media company. In other words, the publisher creates content for a defined and distinct audience and breaks it into micro-content pieces to be distributed where its audience can be found.

Publishers realized that they would not be able to send users (mainly young people) to their destination sites. The solution is to create minichannels of content to be placed on platforms such as YouTube, Snapchat and other social platforms. These content players (such as CNN, Hearst Media, and others) bring content to consumers rather than bringing consumers to the content.

This will make media companies experts in segmental content creation and dissemination while implementing "far from home" business models.

Collecting Data

One of the weaknesses of traditional sites when compared to Facebook and Google is their lack of user information. The proposed solution is to share data between sites (sometimes even between competing companies) in terms of user information.

This solution will enable the publisher to gain thorough and relevant information about its users, even before a user reaches the site. It will allow advertisers the same targeting capability as the big tribes and stop the leakage of budgets.

The tricky part in this solution is to convince sites and app owners to collaborate with competitors with similar problems. It is necessary to find the right body to conduct a complex process of this type without violating the law and without favoring one side over its competitors.

User Identity

Based on the data sharing solution, you can reach the truly important stage of creating a user identity for anyone entering the site or the app. Based on that unique identity, the publisher can channel relevant content for us as users, and connect us with similar / relevant members. Thus, users' leakage to social could be stopped.

Media companies need action based on these three components. Without such a move, it is hard for us to see how traditional media elements can survive the Great Tribal War.

Chapter Thirty-six

Media companies should get their hands into consumers' pockets.

There is no other choice

Advertising as a major or single business model for media companies and publishers is no longer proving itself valid. Most media companies lose users / readers in favor of social, with advertising budgets also moving in that direction. Advertising budgets that are not directed to social and Google are shrinking. Thus, traditional digital media companies should base their existence on end-user payment revenue sources.

Publishers have three options:

1. Making some of the site's content accessible only to paying monthly subscribers.

The first serious and well-publicized move in this area was the *New York Times*, whose print edition, like all newspapers, was in trouble. Consequently, they blocked parts of its website with a "payment wall" that required a consumer to pay in order to read more than a few articles. Many were skeptical about the success of changing their traditional business model, but it soon became clear that millions of Americans were willing to pay for free exposure to the paper's content in its digital edition.

It seems that the press is ripe for a business change of this kind. More or less similar to the change in the music industry based mostly on monthly subscription fees.

2. Opening **digital stores** or marketplaces that offer products relevant to the media company's target audience.

Traditional players such as Hearst Media have launched an e-commerce activity promoting the sale of products of different categories. Publishers now have to reach into their readers' pocket. There is no other option and it can work if they are able to offer a true mix of products and leverage their brand and the data they have about their customers.

3. Developing services and content that are natural for **consumers'** payments (dating, games, music services or sports).

By implementing such a product strategy, publishers can create an additional layer of fixed and stable revenues independent of the (harsh) competition typical of the advertising market in recent years.

Model changing is essential for the survival of publishers.

Chapter Thirty-seven

Social and Content Marketing

Strategies and Implementation

The Triple Strategy of Content Marketing Management

Being aware that the power has shifted to the consumer and that brands need to create value for him in order to build a relationship that will lead to a business-marketing dialog, brands are quickly moving (not necessarily professionally) to Content Marketing activity, which is called: **Inbound Marketing**.

What is content marketing?

Content Marketing addresses the creation and distribution of relevant and valuable content for a defined target audience with the clear goal of attracting and gaining its attention and building a long-term relationship that can eventually turn into a business one.

What are the business goals?

1. Awareness of the company brands

2. A relationship that supports consumer loyalty

3. Differentiation of the brand's products / brands

4. Customer retention

5. Sell & Upsell

There are three steps in Content Conversion

1. The introduction stage

At this stage, the brand offers its potential customers content and information based on its initial acquaintance with them. This stage is characterized by a negligible commitment on the part of the consumer and low involvement. This stage includes in many cases YouTube's brand channel, blog, podcast, interviews and tutorials.

75% of interactions related to content marketing end here, in the introductory stage.

2. The basic bonding stage
This stage is a deeper one in terms of the dialog with potential customers and includes activities such as social friendship and followers, invitation to demo or webinar, as well as subscription to content products such as newsletters.

22% go through this stage of a slightly more in-depth familiarity with the brand's content.

3. The opportunity stage

Only 3% of those who initiated the content process reach a trusting relationship that enables a market-business dialog. This stage includes steps such as "contact" and actual purchase.

How does the triple strategy of Content Marketing management work?

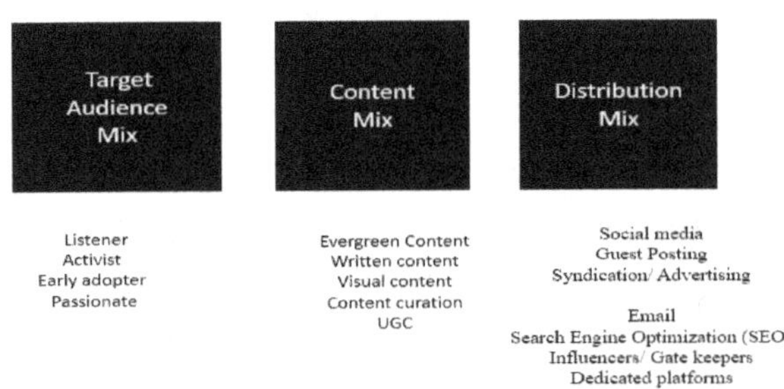

Target Audience:

When planning a marketing move based on strategic entry into the content field, it is necessary to define the target audience in such a way that will improve the chances of success. The combination of proper social networking activity and familiarity with the brand's digital asset, users, will enable the brand to find the right audience for this content activity.

The right audience should at least be a "listening audience" who is willing to watch or read the brand's content. If we can find and create a dialog with an active audience and / or those who are early adopters of ideas and products similar to the brand, they are also likely to be active in creating the content and conveying it throughout their social environment.

The optimal target audience is **the Passionates** who have a passion for the category. Those who are aware of any new relevant content which is uploaded to the network, add it, distribute it and talk about it on and off social. This is the desired goal of any brand starting a real content marketing strategic activity.

Content mix:

A brand that strategically addresses the content area is required to have a true mix of content which consists of five main content types.

1. **Evergreen Content** – relevant content that can be used by the brand every few weeks or months.

2. **Snackable Content** – if you create written content – make it short. This type of content can be easily produced by the

brand's content personnel keeping it original and relevant.

3. **Video/ Visual** content is also important for a dialog with the younger generation to ensure sufficient user collaboration.

4. **UGC** – Content produced by users is necessary for any content or community platform. It is attractive, wins a higher reliability score than some traditional content, and gains a high level of collaboration.

5. **Content curation** – using third party content which is relevant and valuable.

Content distribution mix

Social networks of any kind (Facebook, LinkedIn, YouTube, Twitter, etc.) are the most important tool for distributing branded content. These platforms enable the brand to locate its right audience, broadcast its content and track its performance in the interaction with its target audience.

In addition, the brand has a variety of options for distributing content – email marketing, working with Influencers and micro-Influencers, dedicated content platforms such as Outbrain and programmatic campaigns to promote content and, of course, smart organic search engine optimization.

Every content activity needs to be measured – same as how the market measures the performance of advertising campaigns.

What do you measure?

- Brand exposure
- Interaction with brand content
- Conversions A (from people to visitors) / B (conversion from visitors to friends or followers) / C (conversions from friends to active customers) / D (converting people to being your brand's promoters).

Quality and relevant content can help the brand move the potential customer through all the required steps – from his first entry and exploration stage through the friendship stage up to the marketing-business dialog one.

The new marketers are increasingly adopting new market thinking based on insight:

Think like a publisher

Some brands create only **product-centered** content, with its advantages and benefit. Some brands have risen to the level of **added value** content – namely, information about how the product and its environment can improve, add to or change the life of the customer, including additional features (e.g. a food company offering a recipe application and advice).

Brands that have made the content area their strategic anchor have implemented a **peripheral content** approach – content that is not directly or indirectly related to the product, but rather a new content field that may be of interest to the brand's target audience. For example: Redbull took ownership of Extreme Sports. It has nothing to do with the company's original product; instead they sought to connect to a desired target audience through continuous, professional and differentiated content activity.

One way or another – there is no brand, small or big, that can afford to avoid the strategic area of Content Marketing.

Chapter Thirty-eight

Launching a Brand Zone on Social Network – How do you do it?

Brand presence on social is a necessity, and not only on one social network. Consumers now live on a number of social networks, so the brand has no choice but to live there as well. The goal is to live and not just to create a campaign. If a brand is looking to initiate a relationship with potential customers, it has to produce a value-based dialog which can be done only on social.

If you are a big brand or a small business, there is no way around it – you have to set up your own social zone or page on social. Without this strategic move, effective marketing activity is not possible.

There are a number of steps that need to be implemented in order to launch a brand zone or presence on social:

1. Profile / Target Audience
At this initial stage, the characteristics of the target audience should be defined: who they are, where they spend their digital time, what influences them, whom they influence, what their needs are, what their concerns are, what their media consumption profile is, what their areas of interest are.

2. Triggers
This step defines the triggers which could work for the activity manager / content manager and direct the content on what he should focus on.

There are five trigger types:

- **Information** – news, research in the relevant field, articles, advice, etc.

- **Knowledge** – gossip on the industry, anecdotes and the like

- **Community** – connecting people with similar interests

- **Thrill & Entertainment** – games, humor, and the like

- **Practical benefits** – business opportunities, coupons, discounts and the like

Brands should choose 1-3 triggers that will lead the ongoing content plan of the brand's social presence on each network.

3. Success Parameters
After defining the target audience accurately and laying the foundation for the content we are going to focus on, we should define what we would consider as success. In other words, what the parameters for success are and what factors are to be measured continuously throughout the brand's social activity: visitors, friends, brand followers, comments, sharing, user-generated content, conversion rates from friends to customers, brand awareness and social networking activities, and so on.

4. Launching-penetration activity
Assuming we have done everything right so far, this is the point in which we need to decide how to bring enough people to discover our brand's social zone. This is the stage where we define and plan the launch of our page. It could be a game, campaign or collaborating with other relevant companies that will prompt a significant mass of people to visit our arena.

5. Ongoing management

After the launch, it is time to manage and monitor our activities, performance and planning over time as well as our promotional brand campaigns on social.

This step is done using a simple table called:

Channel Management Template – CMT.

Each row in the table refers to one week and notes the title of the weekly activity, the description of the activity, cost of production, cost of media (if there was budgeted activity), performance – members, exposed, followers, feedback, sharing etc. and finally – decisions, whether to repeat this activity again in the future or not.

We recommend creating a social presence / zone for each micro-segment chosen by the brand, and target and envelop the social zone with complementary digital assets – site, blog, mobile application, bot etc. All the brand's digital assets should support each other, with promotion activities as well as with content exchange between platforms.

Chapter Thirty-nine

How to create the best brand content on social

The past few years saw changes in the way we consume content. **This area of content consumption and media impact is divided into three main generations**:

The Programmed Age – the time when we would learn almost everything and acquired our knowledge through the traditional media.

The Age of Searching – Google has changed the way we absorb content and collect information. Their promise was to provide an answer to our search within 200 milliseconds. People did not have to use media companies to learn about products, services, trends, culture etc.

The Age of Discovery – the current generation. Less pulling of information, more reliance on the social ecosystem – all the content and information we need reaches us as we move through social networks.

This age of content and information consumption requires brands and companies of every kind to integrate into social and join the new dialog. Thus, businesses should adopt publishers' way of thinking and specialize in creating and editing content. In other words – provide the digital natives with real value.

Types of interactions / activities that generate response and interest:

Discounts and sales

Tips

Competition

Humor

Response-generating questions

Utility recommendation

Inspiring quotes

Link to an interesting article

Quiz / Voting

Interesting statistics

The triangle of brand's posting / activity on social:

Effectiveness:

Maximum 3 lines of text

At least 5 times a week

At relevant hours – based on familiarity with the behavior profile of the surfers

Attraction:

Friends' value

Brand positioning as a problem solver

Exclusive information / unique product

Engagement:

Encourage interaction – give users a reason to promote your content

Initiating action

Dissemination of user / follower's content

Timing

The best time to post – About 60% of posts are uploaded between 10 am and 4 pm during business hours. After 4 pm, there is a marked drop in new posts of most brands. However, companies that publish posts outside working hours (early morning and at the end of the business day) have received 20% more interaction from users.

Best Post Day – 86% of posts are published between Monday and Friday, with the interaction index rising 18% on Thursdays and Fridays. In general, the best days for interaction depend, of course, on the area of activity or the brand's category:

Entertainment – The interaction index rises on the weekend, but brands are not active these days, so you should use a pre-made schedule to publish your posts.

Media – Saturday and Sunday are the best days for posting, so avoid advertising on Mondays.

Retail – Users' activity skyrockets on Sundays, yet brands advertise only 5% of their posts at that time. On the other hand, many of the posts are published on Friday when there is a significant decrease in user interaction.

Automotive category – users' interaction is high on Sundays, yet brands advertise only 8% of posts on that day.

Business and finance – most of the posts are published between Monday and Friday, but the indices only rise on Wednesdays and Thursdays.

Fashion – Users' interaction peaks on Thursday, with Friday showing a marked decline in the indices.

Food & Beverage – of all industries surveyed, the interaction of surfers here is much higher than average on Tuesdays and Wednesdays.

Health & Fitness – the interaction index rises on Thursdays.

Sports category – the interaction index rises on the weekend.

Travel and hotels – the lowest interaction index is on Wednesdays, with the highest on Thursdays and Fridays.

How should a brand react to negative user behavior on its social zone / page?

A few basic recommendations regarding negative behavior which appear on your social pages:

- Record-tracking “serial attackers”.
- Do not delete – people identify brutal deletions, a phenomenon that may harm the credibility of the brand.
- Do not delay a response – timing is of the essence when it comes to responding. Explain, but don’t apologize.
- Respond responsibly – do not enter into fights but respond in a way that is based on knowledge and in-depth information on the product / service or the relevant interaction with customers.
- Make sure where the message source is a “kidnapped media” – there are competitors who use your social to attack your brand. In most cases, competitors’ messages appear to look alike so that negative reputations can be identified and so messages can be labeled as undesirable sources (these should be blocked).

In terms of organizing – professional entry into the worlds of content requires the investment of proper and professional manpower – content managers, writers, editors and community managers. This investment will justify itself in the future. A brand should live where its potential customers spend most of their time.

Chapter Forty

Brands need to move from a "brand story" approach to a value-based branding approach

For many years, advertising agencies have claimed that a brand should "tell a story". In other words, "Bring us a fat production and advertising budget so we can invest it in a movie full of dancers that will help us tell the story of the brand."

Now imagine the following scenario: I am a 45-year-old male, interested in natural products – vitamins, supplements, magic powders and natural care products. Every product that comes out, every research published, every newsletter I read, makes me the happiest man on earth. Of course, I downloaded the app of a certain drugstore chain and I follow the brand activity on social networks and blogs.
Now, let's say that the drugstore chain does a good job with big data and knows everything there is to know about me – what I buy, how often, what products, what categories, what my average spending per visit is (digital or offline), what the average time I spend is on each visit to the brand's digital assets.

Knowing all that, they personally remind me to buy vitamin C (they know I take it every day and the last purchase was made almost three months ago). At the same time, they also offer me protein powder for elderly athletes at 50% off and a natural face cream at a nice discount of 30%, everything with a same day delivery.

In other words – they **learned** my needs; they **listened** to me and **delivered a personal value** at the right time, with a unique and tempting sales offer.
I ended up feeling very pleased and really did not miss the graceful dancers from the video ad who were supposed to tell the "brand's story".
In terms of **targeting – listening – relationship – value**, there is no need for all those whistles and bells.

I assume that my creative friends will say that the megalomaniac ad is important in terms of brand support. Well, probably not anymore. The branding process, in most categories, is done more correctly and in a measurable manner by providing a constant value for the consumer.

A value-based brand building is not new and certainly not far-fetched: notice how Google built their brand, and how Facebook did it. All the smarter digital players built their brands by

providing clear and continuous value without investing in grandiose marketing campaigns. This is the main feature of the new branding world – a world in which brands need to characterize, define and locate an accurate target audience, one that is willing to **listen** to what the brand has to say and mainly what it has to **give**.
When it comes to the young digital generation – not only do they not consume linear television, they also do not want to listen to "brand stories".

Chapter Forty-one

Content is still the king. However, the king's clothes are entirely new.

Examining the development of the media shows it has definitely moved from order to somewhat chaotic.

Once the world was organized – there were several content sources that spoke to many recipients. Everyone knew his place. There were a number of newspapers, a few radio and television stations, and a mass of people who learned almost everything from them. The digital world has shattered that familiar order.

The new order arranges content and information in a configuration of **Many to Many**.

Everyone talks to everyone, everyone affects everyone, and everyone is influenced by everyone. The new order also introduced brands that have realized that the only way they could initiate real marketing moves was to develop a relationship with customers and users. The only way to do it is to create value for them. In other words – provide them with relevant, unique, attractive content.

This is why brands have no choice but to think like publishers.

How do you do that? Where do you start? It is customary to consider four layers of activity.

1. **Content Operations**

The organization should be prepared in terms of structure, sources of investment, budgeting, training and recruitment of suitable personnel.

2. **Content Strategy**

As in any market move, here too, there is a need to create a strategy: what kind of content will be relevant to your target audience while at the same time connecting it to your product? Who is the target audience for your content? What does he like? What motivates him? What are his needs? What are his interests and motivations? What is his digital profile? What are his consumption habits?

3. Structure, source and content technology

Are you going to produce the content yourself? Will you use aggregation technologies? How are you going to distribute your content?

4. Measurement / Analytics

In content much like in digital advertising, whatever cannot be measured is not really managed.

What do you measure? How do you measure it? How often? What will be your yardstick for success? All these should be agreed upon as the first step.

We believe that the new strong content players will come from brands. They have no choice and they have the money (unlike the traditional content players, most of which are in financial trouble). Some brands around the world have already begun taking that seriously:

Redbull has long ceased to be just a drink. It is the world's leading publisher in the field of extreme sports – including magazines, apps, sites and extensive activity on social networks.

Nike is not just selling clothes and shoes anymore. This brand has become a sports culture agent and has taken ownership of running and runners, providing them with apps and videos as well as a variety of content such as running tracks, recipes for athletes and tips from experts.

American Express developed a content and community brand for small businesses which are in trouble and need marketing consulting, financial accompaniment, business collaborations, and mentoring in advertising and marketing.

Big brands have an existential need to develop relationships with potential customers and consumers. This need can be satisfied using an effective content marketing strategy.

Add to this the fact that these companies have more resources than the weakening media companies, and you get a new picture of the content and media industry.

A picture in which some of the traditional media players give way to brands that behave and think like publishers.

Chapter Forty-two

Main benefits of Influencers Marketing

The Internet is not highly democratic; there are those who are worthy and those who are worthier – mainly those who have more readers, more followers, more influence and higher access to significant audiences.

Those who are in continuous and substantial contact with a relatively large number of users are sometimes called **Gatekeepers or Influencers.**

What characterizes the relationship between the Influencers and their audience?

Mostly listening. In the digital world, in order to tell a story, convey a message or sell a product and idea, the first step is to fight for the attention level of your target audience. This is no easy feat: evidently, TV advertising does not gain a significant level of attention. Certainly not when it comes to the most important audience today – the Y-Z generations – the digital natives.

Banners also do not enjoy significant attention (remember, 26% of users have already installed ad blockers).

Emotional Engagement is the second characteristic of the relationship between Influencers and their audience.

Many brands have removed any elements associated with traditional advertising from their marketing plans, leaving only social marketing, Influencer marketing, and in field promotion activities.

This mix does not fit all brands of all categories but it's definitely a formula that works great for brands that do it right. Influencers who are associated with the brand, or at least behave as such, connect their readers to the brand, to the content and value it generates.

Which Influencers do you wish to connect to?

Surprisingly, or not, the more targeted and smaller the audience, the better the engagement performance it brings to the brand marketing activity.

Instagram is a very popular platform among Influencers. It is a vibrant platform and highly suitable for recruiting a new audience, as well as being friendly in terms of exposure of elements related to the Influencer himself and the brands with which he works.

However, this is not the only effective platform: people with a significant number of Facebook friends can be an excellent solution, as well as YouTubers with popular channels. Young content creators who are passionate for a certain category create videos for consumers who are likewise passionate about the same category.

It is not clear how long these young media brands will last, but it is an amazing phenomenon brought on by digital platforms such as YouTube and other networks.

These are the young members of the Z generation who enabled independent media empires to generate quite a bit of revenue and at the same time become an excellent alternative for brands that are looking for real presence on the network.

How do you get to the right Influencers?

Influencers' search engines have turned into a marketing and research tool with which you can reach the right Influencers for you on any platform.

What makes Influencers such an attractive marketing tool in the digital age?

Influencers are first of all people who are passionate about the brand, the product and the category. Based on their genuine passion they could promote brands and amplify its message. Their other advantage is attracting audience attention, that same audience which is itself passionate about the category. These are **attentive circles of audiences** who will try your product, talk about it, read your content and distribute it.

Why is that good?

A certified high valued source affects an audience more than a message from a brand or company and affects the readiness to try a new product, listen to the brand and even support or reinforce a buying decision.

Influencer marketing – key benefits

- **Relevance**

The Influencer positions your brand to your audience in a more relevant context.

- **Authenticity**

The Influencer works in a two-way message system and generates trust and attention.

- **Effective Reach**

The digital age is typified by the need to achieve effective reach (as opposed to basic reach in the offline era). Influencers are the most efficient source of effective reach. They do not talk at people. They talk to people they know and their real acquaintance with the audience is a necessary condition for listening.

- **Micro Budget**

Influencers could be used on long, focused tail activity. Business and payment model can be based on per-exposure payment or per-measured post-payment. **Long tail sharing**

research shows that Influencers' audience is more inclined to distribute and share content they get from the Influencer (even if it is a branded content – as long as it brings them value).

Selecting the right Influencers for your brand:

1. Basic adjustment

The basic factors to consider are the match between the identity of the brand, its characteristics, the story it tells, its audience and the consumer's / reader's profile.

2. Interaction-based adjustment

One must take into account the nature of the relationship between the Influencer and his target audience, how involved they are and how tight and frequent their interaction is.

3. Style fit

Media data should also be taken into account, formatting and design, whether it's a YouTuber, Vlogger (a person who regularly posts short videos to a vlog.), textual blog, and so on.

4. Selection based on a business model and measurement capability

One of the advantages of digital marketing is that measurement is done on the fly. This capability should also be maintained when working with Influencers.

Chapter Forty-three

Influencers marketing evolution – brands are looking for micro-Influencers

Brands and businesses are starting to move from Influencers to micro-Influencers. It makes sense.

How to work with micro-Influencers

1. Tell a story based on the value you bring to the target audience.

Your best Influencers are those who are already using your product and preferably those who are Passionates for the category. You should provide your relevant Influencers with an interesting brand story and visual materials that tell your story. This is the right way to turn the Influencer into a brand promoter.

2. Try to achieve continuous presence.

A one-time presence is perceived as campaign. Continuous presence could initiate a relationship with the Influencer's target audience. (Second tier relations).

How to find micro-Influencers?

- You should start with your company's followers. Some of them can become your brand's promoters.

- A small social campaign can help you locate the relevant Influencers.

- Locating working tools with micro-Influencers, for example: https://ninjaoutreach.com/

When you work with small Influencers you are guaranteed success in terms of KPI – **Key Performance Indicator:**

A few differences between mega-Influencers and micro-Influencers:

Mega-Influencers:

- Average number of followers – 2 million
- Average cost per post – 25,000-50,000 USD
- Low involvement
- Moderate listening

Micro-Influencers:

- Average followers – 8,800
- Average cost per post – 500-300 USD
- Higher engagement
- Optimal listening

The digital world invites us to think small (with big potential) in terms of the truly important triangle of: **Micro-Segment/ Micro-Publishers/ Micro-budgets**. This triangle's sides are the most recommended guidelines of your marketing activity.

Define your micro-segment, approach it by using micro-publishers (Influencers and Gatekeepers) and base your marketing on micro, measurable budgets.

The end of mass marketing is here.

Chapter Forty-four

The institutionalization of Influencer marketing

As mentioned above, Influencer marketing is a logical, economic and fundamental trend which has proved effective.

Born a few years ago and much like any other media and marketing area, it has risen up from the bottom – individuals who created content attracted the attention of more and more readers and viewers, later gaining the attention of brands and businesses who have identified among these small media the possibility to gain effective reach at reasonable costs.

During its initial years, campaigns and marketing moves were conducted sporadically, almost unobserved by the super brands and the major media players.

The past year has witnessed increasing signs of the maturation of the field. The key indicator of the relatively rapid institutionalization of the Influencer marketing sector is the launch of tracking, detection and management platforms, which are turning this industry more professional and orderly.

All this is mainly true of marketing activity of Influencers on Instagram, the fastest growing network nowadays – both in terms of users and the number and professionalism of the Influencers.

What should a good platform provide in this area?

1. Accurate targeting – location-based targeting (up to city level), time-based targeting, keyword-based targeting, performance-based targeting (e.g. testing only those Influencers with a minimum of 10,000 targeted listeners and no more than 30,000).
2. A platform that allows the brand to manage records including history of advertising activity divided into performance and costs.
3. A management platform and campaigns should be based on a learning machine that tracks and improves over time with the addition of more and more campaigns.
4. An industry and sub-industry-based search engine.
5. A friendly customer management system – tracking posts, post-performance, and priority-based content planning upload.

6. A dashboard for self-management, which combines the selection of Influencers, from launching the campaign to the measurement and optimization stage.
7. Revaluation of content quality – there is a difference between good content and inspiring content which sustains brand-to-consumer relationships.

The popularity of networks such as Instagram, as well as the understanding that Influencers marketing is a good and effective move, caused the flooding of detection, tracking and management platforms in the market.

My assessment is that, with time, not all players will continue to exist, as a mature market tends to dilute itself and clean up the lesser players or those who have failed to establish a valid business model (while you are reading this, some platforms are already dying out; that is how the digital age operates – companies and enterprises have a relatively short life cycle).

Here are a few examples of platforms that focus on managing Influencers on Instagram:

Heepsy

https://www.heepsy.com

Revfluence
https://www.revfluence.com

Shoutcart
https://shoutcart.com/

Ifluenz
http://www.ifluenz.com/

Famebit
https://famebit.com/

Instabrand
https://openinfluence.com/

Hypetap
www.hypetap.com

TapInfluence
www.tapinfluence.com

Neoreach
https://neoreach.com/

Speakr
https://speakr.com/

Chapter Forty-five

Personalization as a tool for successful Content Marketing

A company or brand that makes a decision to enter the necessary field of content-based marketing should also implement an approach and technologies for personalizing content. Submitting different content to different people based on familiarity with their needs, interests, content consumption and their digital profile (e.g. how likely they are to be involved in your content and even distribute it to their friends). Personalization is based on information gathering processes about potential users as part of the Big Data strategy of the brand or company.

The most important benefits for a brand that steps into content-based marketing activity are organized on seven layers:

Content Contribution Flow

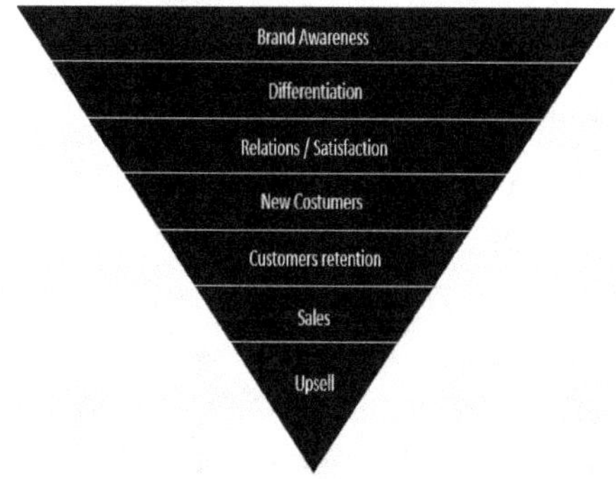

The transition from one stage to the next involves increasing the familiarity with the brand, the content producer, the target audience and creating personal initiatives both in terms of character as well as content and its distribution channels.

The bottom steps of the content-based dialog funnel cannot exist without exact matching of content to the chosen target audience – its economic situation, needs, interests and consumer profile, both digitally and offline.

How do we achieve this level of exact personalization?

1. Activity on social will allow us to "mark" our relevant audiences.

2. First Party Data – This is the brand's data collection activity on our sites and apps. We will do that through registration buttons, bounce technologies that are integrated into our digital assets and, of course, an ongoing and friendly dialog with visitors to our assets.
3. Third Party Data – A database that can be bought or received from third parties who can provide relevant data for our content or business activities.

There are four typical methods for "data collection":

BDM – Behavioral Data Marketing
Players who collect data on the behavior of users. For example, Amazon holds valuable information about consumers' behavior – what they buy, where, from whom, how often, what products, AOV (Average Order Value), APF (Average Purchase Frequency), etc.

IDM – Interests Data Marketing
Gathering information on interests and buying intentions. Google is, of course, the leading player in this field.

SDM – Social Data Marketing
Data based on our social activity – what interests us, what we talk about, who we are, whom we influence, who we are influenced by, and so on.

PDM – Personal Data Marketing

Players who collect personal information about users – personal status, age, residence, occupation, etc.

The behavioral data source is the most effective because it catalogues potential customers based on behavior or actual content consumption. Sources that can provide information based on interests and behavior on social could also improve the personalization of .your content

Chapter Forty-six

In the age of automatic marketing – we return to emotional marketing

The past few years saw a shift to automation in marketing and advertising. Terms such as programmatic advertising have become part of brands and agencies' work plans. Content is also beginning to adopt automated creation technologies.

Ostensibly, a picture of a cold and mechanical field that focuses on targeting, performance and analytics is raising its head. Against the backdrop of this trend, a tendency to integrate activities related to emotional marketing, mainly Experiential Marketing, has recently been rising.

Terms such as Engagement Marketing / Experiential Marketing / Event Marketing / Field Marketing are starring once again in brands' work plans – which is good.

This is a marketing and advertising activity aimed at defined audiences, which is supposed to help the brand generate a range of emotions among potential customers that will support goals such as awareness, sympathy, prominence, developing brand-customers relationships, and their tendency to buy.

Why is it good?

Emotions are not totally separate from reason. They direct our logic to those things that we should focus on and interest us. Feelings make people "think with their heart". A brand can take advantage of this tendency in its favor.

- Feelings generate a first impression of the brand or product.
- Feelings motivate goals of remembering and differentiation.
- Emotions also prompt us to think. This is the first step towards engagement and involvement in the brand and its features.

Emotions generate a response. For example:

- Feeling joy makes us want to share. Sharing is the most effective tool in the crowded field of digital marketing.
- Empathy moves us to connect to people. Emotions evoke the need for a community.
- Surprise and fear drive us to seek a promise of a good, safe and protective

element. Brands can be that good element.

- Passion causes the virality of the feeling and the factors attributed to this emotion. Viral marketing is the ultimate dream of any brand and company.

The majority of emotional marketing is conducted in relatively small settings of participants and exposure.

Entering the next phase of emotional marketing – the natural connection to social networking platforms

The proper emotional marketing of a brand connects customers to it and spurs them to generate opinions about the brand and its actions. Therefore, emotional marketing is one of the elements that may improve performance.

Therefore, emotional marketing is one of the features that could improve a brand's **SPOQ Index – Social Proof of Quality**. As we know, people experience, recommendations and reviews affect us more than any traditional ad. Emotions drive people to refer to our brands in an active way and by that to improve brands' SPOQ Index.

When planning emotional marketing, it is best to refer to two axes: the **first** axis – choosing the emotional range, which is relevant to the product and the target audience. The **second** axis deals with the way to assimilate the emotion-based activity in the product, its branding process, choosing the communications messages and, of course, the company's social strategy.

11 relevant emotions for the marketing action

	Product assimil-ation	Integra-tion in branding	Implementa-tion in the advertising message	Implementation in social networking activities
Fear				
Joy				
Surprise				
Trust				
Expectation				
Gratification / satisfaction				
Excitement				
Relief				
Pride				
Security				
Fear				

Chapter Forty-seven

Typology of social users

Listeners

Listeners enter social networks relatively frequently, from different means and platforms. All in all, they are important to advertisers because they generate a lot of exposure on a daily or weekly basis. On the other hand, listeners contribute very little to the community or to the dissemination of messages, content or .agendas

Activists

Social activists are those who go on social, read, react, distribute, share, and try to influence their friends and relatives. They could become brand or content promoters. **They are one of the most important audiences for brands and media companies.** There is no problem locating and marking them – they are active in many groups on few social platforms, they have quite a lot of .followers and friends

Spammers

This audience enters social to work. They have an agenda, a product or service they are looking to promote. They will take every opportunity to spread their interest. Many of them are removed from groups to which they belong, which does not stop them from continuing to work.

One Trick Pony

They will try to teach us one or two things about life, through the relatively narrow prism of their occupation. They have an interest in helping and spreading .knowledge and information

Early adopters (first to join, first to leave)

Not a big audience but **one of the most important for marketers**. They will join new social, be the first to download new applications and to adopt unique products and content that run on the Internet. They are also the first to leave networks that seem old, irrelevant and outdated. Marketers can use this audience as a first distribution engine but should not rely on them for long.

Family man / woman

The family segment of social perceives it as a family meeting place where family members share their experiences (usually through rose-tinted glasses).

Marketers can reach this audience and try to flood relevant offers. The only way such a move could succeed would be when there is a match between the proposal and the happy life .of the family

The Passionates

This is the most important segment for marketers!!!!

These are people who are passionate about a specific category over time, not as a one-off hit. You are certainly familiar with those who are almost obsessed with cars, fashion, natural and vegan products, extreme sports, travel, computers, gadgets and the like.

Almost every category has a significant micro-segment of Passionates who will try every new product, talk about it, read any content and relevant information, distribute the content to their friends and send feedback. This is the group that could become your best **brand promoters**. Provided that you offer them value relevant to their preferred area.

How do I locate them?

Through social media campaigns, by tracking their search activity on Google and by using direct dialog with them when they reach your site or app.

This is the most effective segment for you.

My recommendation is to invest almost every dollar of your budget in this valuable audience. This is the segment that will provide you with the best ROMI – Return on Marketing Investment.

Chapter Forty-eight

Brand Blog – why is it good and how do you do it right?

A brand or company blog is a digital content area where posts are written and broadcast, posts that describe products, experiences, programs, and any other content that can bring value to a pre-defined audience. This investment is necessary to create differentiation and build a relationship with customers, as well as allow the possibility for the brand to take ownership of a domain or category.

Why is it important to enter this content area?

1. A blog is an additional pillar in the relationship infrastructure the brand builds with its customers. Without creating value, no relationship can exist between brand and consumers, and without a real, ongoing relationship, there can be no effective marketing system.
2. A blog allows the brand to paint itself as an authority in the relevant area.
3. Differentiation – the world of content has become necessary in creating a difference between players in the same field.

4. A smart blog improves the search performance of the brand. It is well known that branded, up-to-date, relevant and original content gets higher scores on Google and other search engines.
5. An interesting and relevant blog improves brand performance in the field of:

SPOQ – Social Proof of Quality – the rising category that addresses all types of people reviews, recommendations, shared experiences and post-purchase feedback. SPOQ leads the new trend of Social Shopping (Products & Services) where the impact of people on our purchasing decisions is much more significant than that of advertising. Where there is attractive and interesting content, there are comments, shares and other user activities that generate signals of quality and involvement. Without social resonance of this kind, the brand loses relevance.

Tips for composing a company blog:

- **Industry News** – If your target audience comes from the industry, familiarize yourself with all relevant information on that industry. Create an image of authority.

- **Consumers' worries and concerns** – If your blog addresses consumers, learn about their concerns, needs, and expectations in the specific content area. This is the first step in developing a relationship with your consumers.

- **Customer Success Stories** – Applaud your customers. Quote their stories of success. Provide them with a stage and wait for their feedback and responses and those of their friends. This approach ensures a high degree of engagement.

- **Using Icons / Visualizations** – Your blog is a platform for creating the prominence and uniqueness of your brand. Do not make do with just smart, relevant text. Combine videos, icons and images. Do not forget, the majority of consumers has adopted a visual communication approach in recent years. In addition, video is known to have a higher level of sharing than text.

- **Surveys and votes** – Popular tools that receive high responses and collaboration.

- **Hierarchical writing** – Headlines, Sub Headlines, Text etc. – Google appreciates a friendly structure for readers.

- **"Share" buttons** in strategic locations – let users be the promoters of your content. Do not make it difficult for them to help you.

- **Register button** – invite your users to a meaningful connection. One that starts with establishing an information basis, for example: email, address, phone.

- **Evergreen content** – try to produce content that can be redistributed periodically, which matches more than a specific time point. Such content can be retrieved whenever it is relevant and save creative resources.

- **UGC** – allow a meaningful platform for content. Invite your customers to contribute their own content. This type of content attracts the most interest and collaboration.

- **Combine** as many popular search terms into your posts as possible. Google will help direct organic traffic to your blog.

- **Perseverance** – A company blog should not directly affect the company's bottom line. It is a valuable tool that does not expect a reward.

- **Mobile optimization** – Do not forget that most exposure comes from mobile users.

Chapter Forty-nine

Digital Marketing activities hierarchy

It's (almost) all about users' attention.

In our age, the marketing world focuses on the pursuit of gaining the attention and listening of customers and users.

Traditional marketing has focused for years on issues such as reach, frequency, awareness etc. The digital evolution of recent years has changed the targeting objectives of brands and businesses. The current battle is about the level of attention and responsiveness of your target audience.

High attention Media
It's the central and most important term that should guide you when you are creating your marketing plans. Paradoxically, the more expensive media means gain a lower level of attention and responsiveness.

The most effective and relevant advertising medium for you is the organic format that is closer to what consumers are looking for.

Users-Initiated Ads
is the format provided to us following our search. In other words – after we send a clear signal of intention to buy and interest in the product. Naturally, when we generate a signal of interest, our level of attention is high and the seller's dialog with his customers at this stage is the most relevant and efficient.

On the higher level above this dialog is the layer of activities, related to what other customers have to say about a particular product or service. It is clear that people-influencing-people gains more meaningful attention than advertising where an official message (advertiser) is trying to sell us a product or service. This field, which includes reviews, inputs, recommendations, etc., affects us more than anything else.

SPOQ - Social Proof of Quality
SPOQ refers to all types of people reviews, recommendations, shared experiences and post-purchase feedback and is perceived as authentic, reliable and very efficient at the stage when we are about to make a preference or purchase decision. Brands and businesses can certainly affect this important area. How do you do it? First of all, by creating a genuine relationship with your target audience. Based on it, it is possible to generate organic or promoted motivation (incentives) in clients to

share their experiences with your service or product.

Much has been written about this important and evolving field. Companies and brands now understand that without a relationship with customers, they will have no successful marketing and with no value on the part of the brand, there will be no relationship.

This insight leads most companies to implement a content strategy that puts consumers at the center. Content marketing targets the creation and distribution of relevant and valuable content for a defined target audience with the clear goal of attracting and gaining their attention and building a long-term relationship that can become a business one.

Companies learn to exploit this resource for purposes such as brand awareness, relationship formation, brand differentiation, sales, customer retention, and resale based on customer loyalty.

Companies such as Nike, Walmart, American Express and Redbull have become publishers and invest in creating and distributing content more than they do in any other marketing means.

The coming years will see an increase in the share of this sector in the marketing budget pie of all companies, in any area and any size.

What content will gain attention and create a trigger for sharing?

1. **Content perceived as exclusive** – offer your users unique content or value. A feeling of uniqueness ensures engagement. This could be information, research, or transferable coupons – the point being that the content is perceived as intended for a limited audience to which he belongs.
2. **Visual content – preferably video**. Video content is distributed more than any other format. Video wins 26% more shares than images and about 58% more than text. Any content should be sharable – searchable and snackable.
3. **Gamification** – People love to compete – and win. For example, instead of releasing dry informative content, you can turn it into a trivia game that is easily accessible and simple to use. Presenting the participants' scores on a dynamic and updated table will ensure its distribution – at least by those who end on top.

4. **Dispute** – Branded content that causes emotional debate will gain greater participation and involvement. For example, a dairy producer can post studies showing that milk is a healthy and essential ingredient while trying to counter the argument that milk is fundamentally bad. The debate that will rage around the informative content will ensure high users' engagement, which will also create sharing.
5. **Humor** – preferably as a short video – will win a multi-circular sharing that will do a good job for the brand and strengthen factors such as brand connection, recollection and differentiation.

What else will work for you? Choosing the right Influencers and **micro-Influencers** will also ensure an effective attention level and responsiveness for you. The past year has seen a rise in the field of micro-Influencers as a preferable option.

What are micro-Influencers?

Mainly Social Network activists – who are not celebrities – who have a relationship based on a common interest with a small audience who listens, follows and responds to the Influencer. The size of the population that follows and listens is between 1,000 and 10,000.

Why should I work with micro-Influencers?

They offer more meaningful listening, high involvement, and an effective degree of recollections for each message.

Cross-sectional data shows 60% more involvement with micro-Influencers' content than with high profile celebrities.

Even in terms of managing long-term marketing activity, there is an advantage because the budgets required when working with big Influencers are on average seven times higher.

Another interesting statistic is – there is 22.2% more talk around the content of micro-Influencers.

Why do micro- Influencers produce better engagement data?

The advantage of intimacy and relevance reinforces all the parameters that are important to us as marketers and brands –

proximity, relationship, trust, relevance, authenticity and identification.

The traditional digital platforms (sites and apps) and certainly the traditional offline platforms (television, press, billboards) cannot guarantee you the level of attention necessary for effective dialog with existing customers and potential new ones.

The necessary pursuit for attention and listening parameters invites us to think small (and make it big) in terms of the truly important triangle:

Micro-Segment / Micro-Publishers / Micro-Budgets

or in other words, forget about the term "mass".

| Media Attention Hierarchy

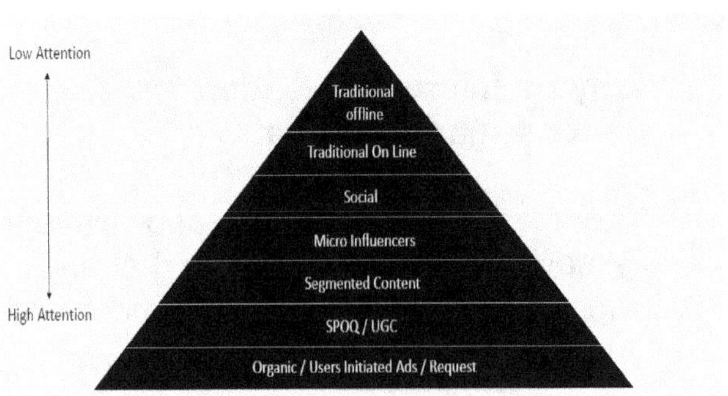

Chapter Fifty

How will SPOQ – Social Proof of Quality – affect Brands and Content Companies?

SPOQ is a super-term that describes all the channels through which people influence others in their purchasing decisions and preference of a product or service. It refers to all types of people reviews, recommendations, shared experiences and post-purchase feedback. SPOQ leads the new trend of Social Shopping (Products & Services) in which the Impact of other people on our purchasing decisions is much more significant than advertising.

Brands and companies realize that they have to address users' responses constantly accumulated on the web as a resource or threat. In any case, no one can ignore the power people hold over our buying intentions and their realization.

The experience of users or buyers is the most significant configuration of UGC – User-Generated Content, in terms of impact on consumer and brand positioning and marketing. A good example of such a company that acts in this field and has already raised tens of millions of dollars is Yotpo https://www.yotpo.com/

The company enables digital stores to manage user experiences optimally, to control the published content and distribute it as a marketing material on social.

How can brands improve their SPOQ Index? How can you manage and maximize this resource? How to set up a marketing plan based on user or customer reviews?

1. This domain operated under the assumption that a relationship with users and potential customers should be built. Thus, an action plan should be built which encourages them to post positive feedback and share their experiences with their friends.
2. Develop as many "feedback zones" as possible on your digital assets, user friendly and easy to use.

3. Invite users and customers to write reviews. In the digital age people tend to write, so ask them to do something they naturally tend to do – share!!!! However, remember – it's important to be personal but not emotional. Emotional appeal is ineffective. A personal approach certainly brings a better response.
4. Initiate **loyalty programs** for registered customers. Reward them for what they write. A reward can be the accumulation of points, an invitation to enjoy a special sale or win a personal benefit.
5. Good reviews are the best advertisement for your business. Distribute them on social. This is the most authentic and influential marketing content. Dynamic ads that include customer feedback get double the clicks and are cost effective.
6. User reviews is the best testimonials-based advertisement.
7. Respond to critics in a practical and constructive manner. Use the dialog to improve your relationship with them.
8. Most importantly, mobile interaction brings more feedback and more sharing. The personal device generates more openness for users and customers to be involved.

You have to remember the winning formula – Fresh, Relevant, Dynamic, Authentic. UGC = better SEO performance.

Chapter Fifty-one

E-commerce. How to make it work?

How to start an independent E-commerce business

The digital natives' generation has changed the labor market – more entrepreneurs with lesser tendency to bind themselves to a corporate workplace.

An interesting, related phenomenon is the growth of the freelance segment in the United States (and worldwide). According to the Freelancers Union 35% of the US workforce, or **55 million** people, are freelancers. This figure is on the rise as a result of the independent entrepreneurial perception common to the labor market of recent years.

At the same time, friendly technologies allow users to move easily from the idea stage to the implementation one, especially in e-commerce, which has seen a rise in all categories, led by fashion, electronics, computers and accessories.

If you are part of this growing segment of entrepreneurs and wish to launch a digital store, here are 10 steps you should take to succeed in your e-commerce venture:

1. **Find product ideas** – follow your passion. Try to focus on selling products or services that are close to your heart. A business area where there is a chance that you will be an expert.

2. **Learn from competitors** – make a comparison chart and find your unique selling proposition (USP).

3. **Learn from community players** – where you can learn about people's taste and potential buyers. A venue where members can add products, build a shared index, and be exposed to the preferences of other inspiring users.

4. **Learn from places which behave as a marketplace in the commerce arena:** https://wanelo.com/

5. **Competitor Research** – product line, product strategy, pricing strategy, site performance (similar web, Alexa), mobile performance (Google Play), performance and activity on social, etc.

Trend Research – it's also a good idea to use Google Trend, to test each of your ideas and check trends and demand: https://www.google.com/trends/

6. **Selecting a primary micro-segment** – focus on the Passionates of the category. Those who try every new product in the relevant industry, those who will talk about your product, and those who will read content and will distribute and share with their friends. This segment of people can be transformed into **brand promoters**.

7. **Product and Price Strategy** – Look for price sensitivity (usually up to $70 is a reasonable price sensitivity).

8. **Establishment**

- Choosing a brand name and logo (it is advisable to register a trademark already at the first stage).

- Simple and fast building of your branded store, using specialized platforms for digital stores, for example: http://www.shopify.com/.

- Create content strategy and anchor features, such as: about the company, product catalogue, payment terms, shipping policy, return policy, store contact options, payment options (use a branded solution like PayPal to remove shopping barriers).

- Operational preparation – inventory (preferably graded and managed accurately), shipping operation, customer service (use of existing chatbot solutions).

- Cross platform presence – site, mobile app store (you can use automated solutions such as https://bobile.com/), purchase options in a social networks store.

9. **Marketing and advertising strategy**
Constructing the program with two objectives in mind:

- Brand building

- Sales / performance

10. **Media strategy – based on response speed:**
- Fast-performance media – social networks, company sites, Influencers, direct marketing (e.g. email marketing)
- Deep media – medium response speed – organic promotion, Google sponsored promotion, content-based marketing activity.

If you do not have a unique and original product and still want to integrate into the value chain of e-commerce, you can do so by working with retailers or importers and other manufacturers or with giants such as AliExpress in a configuration called:

Drop shipping. This is a supply chain management methodology where the digital store does not hold any stock. Here the retailer manages all contact with the final customer, including pricing and shipping, but the product comes from another retailer or the manufacturer who allows access to his products.

Chapter Fifty-two

E-commerce – Six Conditions for Success

The (true) premonitions shared by everyone involved in commerce are that we are approaching the end of the reign of malls. More and more malls in the United States and Western Europe are shutting down and most business owners are channeling their energies and resources into online shopping.

Anyone who turns to e-commerce will find quite a few opportunities and potentials, yet also hurdles which should be considered.

In order for an e-commerce site to succeed, it should operate on two levels:

1. Creating added value (compared to competitors and compared to offline shopping / traditional)
2. A breakdown of barriers

As for added value, it is customary to focus on three elements:

- **Value offers**

Can be targeted at prices and / or offering products and services that are not available through traditional shopping or from the competitors.

- **Social buying**

Creating distinguishing social value between online and offline buying. This can be reflected in customers' sharing their buying experience, buying together or making purchase lists before special events. Amazon, for example, allows discussions before buying books and invites users to choose the gift they want to receive from their friends for their birthday.

- **Shopping experience**

Using technology for shopping experience has become easy and simple. Today, digital stores provide a powerful, personalized, friendly shopping experience.

Each potential customer is offered a different design and presentation based on their preferences and purchasing profile. Customization / personalization are fundamental for the success of digital shops, which did not exist in the era of physical stores. Accessibility is also a major and most effective issue: arranging products by brand names? Organizing the shelf according to sales discount? Arranging products by price? We have all the options available if we have built the digital store correctly and smartly.

To dismantle barriers, three matters should be addressed:

- **Payment**

40% of consumers are still concerned about the malicious usage of their payment tool / credit cards. Sounds strange? Maybe, but if you are not part of the digital generation – the Z and Y generations, you are still not completely worry-free.

What can storeowners do? Make payment to Smart-Simple-Safe. In other words, you can embed tools such as PayPal and allow the user to complete a purchase with one click. One click away from the destination.

- **Shipping**

Many consumers are still worried about shipping: The product might arrive damaged? Might not arrive at all? Not arrive on time? Basic concerns that might suspend purchasing.

What can storeowners do? The solution is control – allow your customer to know where their package is at any given moment. A promise of free shipping can, of course, help... After all we all love this word – free.

- **Return policy – perhaps the most significant impediment**

What to do? Promise and back your promise. Market surveys show that the way to dismantle barriers and worries is to promise. Extreme promise may work.

Extreme case – Zapos was the first to guarantee a return policy of one year from the day of purchase!!!!

To conclude: if you launch an e-commerce / digital store, consider the three components of added value and the three basic barriers that need to be dismantled.

Chapter Fifty-three

How can digital stores fight giants like Amazon?

Amazon's expansion and entry into new markets could be a major threat to local players who are already facing increasing competition from global online shopping alternatives. The threatened players are those in the most active categories in the local market:

58% of shoppers online are going for fashion
38% are looking for smart phones and related products
37% for gadgets and games
35% for beauty products

A major entry of a giant such as Amazon to the local market could wash away the chances of survival of local players in these leading areas.

How can they survive?

Me Too strategy – as strange as it sounds the right way is to assimilate an appropriate strategy, while maintaining a local specificity relevant to the local community. Only thus will local players be able to maintain relevance and gain advantages and sporadic market victories.

What does all this mean?

Create a package of services and added-value products for customers. Just like Amazon does. Bundling, but with local uniqueness.

Let's say you have a fashion store. How is it supposed to look?

- **Express Delivery** – Free. In a few hours, the package lands on your doorstep.
- **Exchange Policy** – You have 8 weeks to decide whether you wish to keep the product (clear and defined terms for return).
- **Content packages** – Advice, styling, fashion shows and the like. Everything that can interest those who buy from your fashion store from time to time. This component in your package will be part of a cooperation with relevant content companies.
- **Effective technologies – for example, virtual reality** that allows everyone to try on and experience the store's products before buying.

- **Early bird sale offers** for prime customers only
- **Micro-segmental strategy** and creating targeted product lines for local customers, including group bundling.
- **Collaboration with local stores** with complementary products – when you buy from one partner in the "package" you get a 10% discount, from two partners, you are entitled to a 20% discount, and the third partner entitles you to a 30% discount.
- **Branded cash** – develop your own digital currency (can be based on token technology but not necessarily). Reward customers for visiting your properties (store, website, app, blog). Make sure you award your customers a coin for every visit or sharing of content or distribution of a product. The more their wallet is filled up with your branded coins, the more involved they will be in your brand.

Of course, you cannot offer the exact same package as Amazon does – music, books, cloud services etc. Yet with some creativity and assimilation of the same concept, even small players, local and high quality, will win this war.

Chapter Fifty-four

A Digital store – Chatbots instead of salespeople

A Chatbot – or bot – is actually a computer program that performs an automatically defined task. Bots can provide you with information from various sources, can answer your questions, advise you, and of course, help you with an efficient and swift online purchasing process.

E-commerce has developed in recent years in terms of supply, friendly use and consumer willingness to be part of this revolution. In order to succeed in digital business of this type, two objectives related to consumer behavior should be met:

Keep it smart-simple-safe

Give your potential consumers the feeling they are enjoying a smart service that knows all about them, reaching each and every one with a personalized offer. Try to give your consumers the feeling that everything is simple, accessible, friendly and safe.

The digital generation, primarily the Z and Y ones, are attracted to efficient stores with the option of **one click away from purchasing (and in some cases zero clicks purchasing)**. The ideal platform for that is smart bots. Last year's studies showed that young people tend to buy from branded bots that simplify the purchase process.

If you run a digital store or plan to initiate one, the optimal way to acquire customers is to integrate a bot-based solution into the dialog chain with your customers.

Another thing that will promote your business is combining special offers and coupons as part of your main selling reach. The Z generation is in love with the concept of personal digital coupons.

Beyond the perceived attractiveness of bots is the considerable information they gather about the user, his purchasing practice, his shopping tendencies, and more. Substantial data to help you better plan your product and marketing strategy.

Chapter Fifty-five

Is your site or store performance poor?

A few tips for improving traffic

The last decade saw companies of different types and sizes which have understood the need to create a presence in the digital world. Digital presence can no longer do with just a website. The company must create a whole spider of digital assets adapted to its target audience and the nature of its activity. Digital natives live simultaneously on different platforms. A brand wishing to attract their attention has to position itself at all of those relevant crossroads – destination site, social platforms, mobile, blogs and so on.

Construction of these digital assets has in recent years become automated, easy, convenient, cheap and fast. Companies such as Wix or WordPress (web site development) as well as Appsvillage and Bobile (mobile development of mobile applications) are accessible to any entrepreneur or marketer.

Still, attracting customers, creating awareness, retaining and returning customers, has become complex and dense. The main battle of companies and app owners is aimed at attracting our attention.

One of the most basic and complex tasks is to create organic traffic to your site.

Here are some guidelines:

- First and foremost, learn and update the researched key words and anchor words in your field, continuously. In other words, what words do people use when searching for a product / service of your category? Learn these words, even if you have no intention of "buying" words and getting involved in bidding (which costs money).
- Use standard language to create web pages and web applications. Language that Google can identify.
- Make sure that some anchor words appear in your domain.
- Invest in content. A lot. Content that is relevant to your customers, up-to-date content, dynamic and original content. Google will appreciate that and place you in a good position on its search.

- Use the anchor words a lot, sensitively. Make sure they appear in the first 100 words on your home page.
- Use multimedia – images, video, and animations, as much as possible, making sure these are relevant to your target audience.
- Be user-friendly with the right hierarchical structure, which makes sense, using numbering and bullets.
- Mobile optimization – important. Do not forget to do it during your site's development stage.
- Set up a YouTube channel (if relevant). Google appreciates that very much.
- Include UGC – User-Generated Content that improves your position in search results. Customer reviews, feedback, remarks, recommendations and social comments.
- The longer the average time spent on your site, the higher your score from Google. If you have content that generates involvement, you are good to go.
- Directing traffic to your site increases your chances, so it's a good idea to invest in collaborations with relevant sites and possibly together with your own campaigns.

This list can be the promotion work plan for every site.

Other brand assets will also have to prepare a clear and practical plan. The way to create a relationship between the brand and its customers goes through a successful digital asset set.

Chapter Fifty-six

Social Commerce

An indispensable layer in E-commerce activity

E-commerce is becoming part of everyday life for consumers and business / brand owners. Accessibility, product visualization, segmentation, differentiation and personalization are cornerstones of this evolving industry.

There is one additional significant layer that changes the rules of the game for the supplier and that is customer sales dialog. That layer is the social and / or community characteristics that affect the customer's shopping journey and the way he gets purchase decision.

This additional layer is called: **Social Commerce**.

Here is a very basic and familiar example: If friends on Facebook hit Like to the song I uploaded, some of them might buy the song.

What is the role of these social elements in purchasing?

- **Brand's relevance** – based on the information about the way members use the product or feedback about it, I define how relevant it is to me and to my reference group.
- **Pre-purchase hesitation** – just before I buy, I consult with my friends. Sharing with them my last minute thoughts. This can happen in the digital store or across the net.
- **Purchase decision** – the moment of decision. Here too, friends, or friends of friends, the so-called **FOF** can be a factor in the decision process. At this point I influence others based on my own experience. I become an Influencer instead of one of the influenced, even if that influence is not applied to my direct friends.

The digital or e-commerce world cannot exist today without this significant component of mutual influence in the community of users, and without the social characteristics of sales and purchase moves.

Every social activity, across all networks, affects the purchasing campaign of consumers, primarily the digital natives' generation who post purchase feedback.

The age of discovery is the term that describes the first stop on the digital consumer's shopping journey. Unlike previous stages, where we learned about products and located them through the traditional media, and later on with search engine optimization, current times are characterized by gathering global information (including locating products) while hanging out on social.

This is the first and basic layer of the field called **Social Commerce**.

Nearly 40% of millennial users reported that their first encounter with relevant products was on either Facebook, Instagram or Pinterest. The more the network is characterized as a "visual media area", the more it plays a significant and effective role in the interaction between users and a new product.

In the United States, the majority of those who start their shopping journey on Facebook end up with Amazon. The brand's home page is second to the completion of their shopping campaign, which has started on social. The past year has witnessed a correlation between the beginning of the journey on Facebook and shopping on social, as well as traffic to the physical store of the brand. The cross-platform acquisition concept becomes strategic for brands and companies that understand the importance of social strata to promote their digital sales.

Another role of the social layer lies in allowing digital brands and stores to locate and mark the passionate segment into their category. A natural products store can easily use social to pinpoint those who crave natural foods, natural beauty products or unique recipes for the veggies that the store incorporates in its value proposition.

A digital store that focuses its marketing activity in this segment will be able to perform better in Return on Marketing Investments (ROMI). Each invested dollar will work better for the store when it comes to this segment of Passionates; they will try new products, read the content that the store offers, distribute that content to their friends and talk about the store products.

Identifying this target audience and turning it into a brand promoter is perhaps the most significant anchor for the social layer in the e-commerce category.

Chapter Fifty-seven

SPOQ – Social Proof of Quality

The most Important Marketing Vehicle for your Digital store

Imagine yourself on vacation in a country which you have never visited before, looking for a hotel in the city center. There are many options and you are debating which to choose. One of the first steps you take is to scroll down to the bottom of the hotels page to read comments and recommendations of users/ customers.

If their feedback is bad and the hotel's general score is less than 8, you will move on to the next one. This is very much like the way we used to do things for years in the past when we came to a new place and looked for a restaurant for dinner. We never went into an empty restaurant, preferring to stand in line for a table in the restaurant next door which looks full and busy.

This is the meaning of the very significant term: **Social Proof of Quality – SPOQ**.

In the digital age, “social density”, on a positive side, is worth more than any advertising campaign. It is an indicator of quality.

Research shows that 77% of users read customers’ recommendations before making their purchase decision. This figure crosses all categories and characterizes most worldwide locations.

Digital stores should address this data and add users’ feedback as a main vehicle in their ongoing marketing plan.

A good product and service could entice buyers to recommend it to others. It is also possible to send an email to the satisfied buyer and ask him to leave positive feedback or offer an incentive to those buyers who agree to share their good experiences with potential customers. You want to use structured and friendly programs such as: Shopify Discount Code. This simple tool allows digital storeowners to provide customers with these types of benefits:

- Percentage discount
- Shipment discount

Tools such as these are highly effective for triggering (experiences, recommendations, brand-supporting social activities) as well as for setting up and maintaining digital stores' loyalty programs and customer member clubs.

One of the most effective ways to support your SPOQ Index – Social Proof of Quality – is to take ownership of a particular domain by launching and maintaining a professional blog written by the store owner, encouraging customers (preferably in the Passionates' segment) to read, respond, share and produce the signals of social proof of quality.

SPOQ has become important for every digital marketing move:

90% of consumers read customer reviews before visiting the store or the service provider's website.

31% reported that they tend to buy more from a site with good reviews.

72% will make a buying decision only after reading surfers' feedback.

What is the impact of SPOQ on the business / brand marketing activity?

- It essentially creates **user content** in the most authentic and original way. This type of content is famous for attracting a higher level of attention and enjoys better results on organic search engine promotion. Google favors original, dynamic and authentic content.

- **It boosts long tail key word traffic** – users who share their buying experience generally use the same words as potential consumers do in their search (the pre-buying one). The overlap between the words ensures improved organic promotion activity.
- A community scene of this type triggers talk about the brand, products and experience.
- A lively and positive conversation about the brand and its products produces a **signal of relevance**, authenticity and above all reliability which is expressed in terms such as: **Authority and Trusted.**
- A discussion on the brand and the service improves its perceived ranking compared to the competitors.

Work plan for upgrading Brand's SPOQ

1. Encourage users to be involved and share their shopping experience with you. This can be done by direct contact or by encouraging sharing on social. First invite them to be your friends or

followers, then encourage them to be part of your responders' group.
2. Maintain continuous communication with those who have already shared and written. Maintain a public and personal dialog about their feelings and experiences about the brand, including ways to improve it.
3. Initiate a compensation plan for consumers who become active. For those who write and share their experiences about your brand, on your site and on other platforms. Loyalty programs or compensation programs could be part of the strategic plan of any digital site or stores.

SPOQ measurement components:

1. Sentiment – Go over all relevant digital arenas to understand whether the public supports your brand or whether the general sentiment is negative. There could be differences in sentiment between different platforms. For example, brand sentiment may be positive on the brand's destination site while social sentiment (on social networks) is negative.

In this case, you should examine the differences in usage and depth of familiarity with the brand, between customers who entered your store or site, and those exposed to your brand through social.

2. Emotions Volume – to what extent are the negative feedbacks, for example, extreme and decisive. This component can be tested by assimilating semantic tracking technologies that examine words used by surfers. There is a difference between words such as: "I was not happy" or "did not meet expectations" compared to words such as: "disappointment", "crooks" or "poor product".

3. Quantity – The number of respondents and feedbacks. You can simply count the number of responses and responders during a relevant period (usually once a month or a quarter). Examine the number of responses and responders on the various digital platforms. It will certainly be interesting to see the differences between the brand's home page, app, social and external digital channels. A small number of comments and reviews means that the Engagement Index of the brand is not sufficient.

Numerous measurement tools are available on the market with entrepreneurs who develop smart tools to meet this specific goal.

In any case, I recommend that companies and brands invest in developing such an efficient tool. In the coming years, **SPOQ** will become an increasingly significant signal domain for quality based on user experiences.

Chapter Fifty-eight

The winning formula for digital stores

AOV (Average Order Value) & APF (Average Purchase Frequency)

AOV is the average sum of money that a customer spends in a single store in a given period of time.

APF is the number of times an average customer buys goods or services from a specific seller in a given period of time.

These are the two most important components of digital store performance, which should be addressed in order to improve revenue.

Ways to improve AOV performance

1. **Focus on marketing for the passionate segment**

These are people with a defined passion for the category. For example, some people crave fashion on a daily basis. If you run a digital fashion store, you should trace that segment and dedicate most of your marketing energy and resources there. This segment consists of people who are more attuned to messages and content in the category they are passionate about. They will read your content and share it with their friends. They will try new products and talk about them and once they reach your store, they will probably spend more money. The average expenditure per purchase on fashion in digital stores is around $97. The average expenditure of Passionates was almost $126 – 29% higher.

Think about what it might do to your bottom line.

How to find my Passionates? Facebook allows you to target them through their interests and affiliation to the relevant groups. Google allows the use of the search terms they use. You can also take advantage of every visit to your store to invite them to join your community of valued shoppers. They usually accept invitations to sales.

2. Getting to know your target audience, their needs, financial abilities, desires, shopping and spending track record in your store. Knowing your customers' behavior will help you improve your AOV performance.

3. Personal promotions based on a thorough understanding of your customers, while promoting tailor-made offers of complementary or similar products to the products and offers which attracted your consumer to your store in the first place.

4. A personalized store design. One of the significant advantages of digital stores compared to physical ones is the ability to display a specially designed store for every consumer – a store that looks different, displays specific shelves, and focuses on specific products or sales.

Each customer gets a different configuration of the stock based on their personal preferences, needs, and purchase history.

Ways to improve APF performance

1. **Group** Purchasing. Imagine a post – a digital store inviting its members to a "**50 / 50**" campaign – a 50% discount is guaranteed to members if they come to the store as a group of 50 shoppers within a defined period of time. A group purchase guarantees the brand or store its members will work hard to share that promotion in order to guarantee 50 people to come and buy the product. Most of the people who

join have never planned to go shopping but were drawn into it as a result of the sale.

2. **Content**. When you bring value to your customers even when they are not buying, there is a good chance you will lure them to unplanned shopping. Good content improves **contact frequency** between the store and its customers. Contact density is an important factor that leads to a selling dialog.
3. **Business-Oriented Triggers**. These solutions can move people from a place devoid of a sales dialog (the store's Facebook page) to a venue with selling potential (the digital store). Such persuasion solutions can consist of coupons, point accumulation plan, etc.
4. **Family or couples' packages**. If relevant, this is certainly a move that could improve shopping frequency.
5. **Loyalty Programs**. An excellent vehicle that could support shopping volume targets and improve purchasing frequency. Loyalty programs offer real value to customers, motivate them to become returning customers and, of course, prevent customers moving to your competitors.

6. Customer retention campaign. Email, social, mobile – all are good, as long as you create unique value, and a personal and flattering offer.

What should you measure?

Repeat Purchase Rate = The number of buyers who have bought more than once in the past year – divided by the total number of customers in the past year.

Purchase Frequency = the number of orders in the past year – divided by the number of (different) buyers in the past year.

Chapter Fifty-nine

Customer retention in the digital age

A well-known rule states that it is much easier and more efficient to retain existing customers than to recruit new ones, which has to do with financial and management resources.

Every brand or store should set up, not only a proper marketing plan, but alongside it, or as part of it, a plan for retaining existing customers.

Here are some measures and components that should be included in the business plan of every business:

1. **Customer profile map** – Invest your resources in creating an interaction / visits / shopping map for each customer in the past year. The map will provide you with graphic information such as when the customer visits your store, how often he comes, how often he buys, what he usually buys, how much he spends. For the next step, fill in the gaps (the periods without interaction) with complementary products (i.e. night

treatment face cream for those who bought day treatment face cream) or any other content that generates added value relevant to the customer's interests.

That is called Interaction Gaps Offerings – suggestions and content based on an in-depth knowledge map is the most basic and efficient move for customer retention and data leverage.

2. **E-mail-based retention marketing** – which is continuous and focused on tailor-made content for the customer. The e-mail should be focused on content rather than on sale offers. Personal emails should be sent rather frequently but no more than once or twice a month.
3. **VIP Program** – Let customers feel special. A feeling of exclusivity results in high level of attention and allows to bridge interaction gaps effectively.
4. **Control tools** – One of the most important things for customers is their sense of control (of their spending and opportunities). Develop a utility tool that will be available to customers which provides them with a sense of control.

This could be a calculator, an expense management tool or a bot which they could also use for any question or advice.

5. **Cross-Platform Presence** – As part of getting to know your customers, find out in which digital arenas they are active and be there together with them and for them. Let them know that you live in those same arenas. Cross-platform presence is a prerequisite for long-term relationships with potential customers and consumers.
6. Fill in the interaction gaps **with short-term offers** and offers for group purchases.
7. Offer your customers a **reward plan** for becoming brand promoters. People who share your content and promotions and initiate talk about your store or brand are entitled to rewards and personal benefits. Keep in mind that people are more attentive to content and suggestions from their friends than those coming from the store or brand.

Your path to success relies on two main axes – customer acquisition and retention. Two axes for which it is worthwhile to prepare continuous and measurable work plans.

Chapter Sixty

Should digital shops implement a defensive, offensive or creative marketing strategy?

Digital marketing offers many strategic options for online stores, businesses and brands. One of the questions small and large businesses face is whether to initiate an offensive, defensive or creative marketing strategy. The decision does not necessarily have to be kept over time and can be limited depending on the market and the competition.

1. Offensive marketing strategy

The main idea is to attack your main competitor / competitors in their field: focus on their most important target audience segment and come up with a better value than them.

Here you should monitor the sentiment of your competitor's customers – contentment or dissatisfaction – based on SPOQ –

Social Proof of Quality data, as they post it on their respective digital and social.

This initiative could open up an interesting marketing opportunity for you, which is not necessarily related to your product or business advantage over your competitor but stems from the openness of your customers to hear about new possibilities.

2. Defensive marketing strategy

When will a company be required to implement a defensive strategy – temporary or long-term?

Following aggressive moves by a competitor and the desire to retain market share, customer share and existing marketing advantage.

Such a strategy can also be initiated, not necessarily in the wake of a competitor's move, but as a reaction to public criticism of the company or its products. Criticism that appears on digital platforms such as social networks, and which produces **viral public anger** that might sink the brand's assets in a way that calls for a smart defense strategy.

An entry of a new player that implements a Me Too Product and Marketing strategy can also be a good reason to implement a defensive strategy that could help brands keep their position and assets.

3. Creative strategy (not linked to a direct reference to the competitors)
Different is better than better.

Different thinking, different products, another target audience, a completely different business and marketing approach. This strategy is necessary when your area of activity is crowded and packed with value propositions similar to yours.

The first step in this strategy should begin with defining a micro-segment that you wish to concentrate on in your new work plan. The more accurately you target your audience, the more you can customize your products in a way that is suitable and relevant for it, and consequently your marketing penetration program will be more efficient.

Start with a relatively limited and highly focused audience, and gradually expand to wider ones.

Do not be afraid to work with a smaller micro-segment. Only then will you be able to form a genuine relationship with them – a necessary condition for any marketing activity.

The next step is **listening** – you should hear what your audience wants. What motivates it, what its needs are, by whom it is influenced, who it influences, what its adversities are, and what are its consumption habits.

Once you understand all that, it's time to tailor a worthy value package for your selected micro-segment and choose the designated communication channels through which you will reach it.

Overview

Is your digital activity good enough?

The triangle model for a Brand's Digital Activity Evaluation and preparation of brand's digital presence

The developing and dynamic field of Digital Marketing is rich in terminology, methodologies, platforms, technologies, measurement tools, theories, perceptions, insights, with albeit quite a few dilemmas and experiments.

As in any relatively young field, professionals and managers learn on the move trying to understand which business and market decisions will promote and strengthen their company.

Are we doing it right? Are we using the digital arena optimally? Do we really meet the needs and expectations of the digital natives?

The triangles model attempts to answer these and other questions by looking at and

examining five layers of your digital activity:

1. Do you consider the three most important elements when setting up and running your **digital business**?
2. Do you address the main three issues of Digital Marketing?
3. Do you manage to produce a successful social activity based on the three most important aspects of the field?
4. Is your content strategy based on the right anchors?
5. Does your digital store make accurate use of the technological advantages and the right marketing moves?

Here are the five triangles that will help you to better understand the quality of your digital activity:

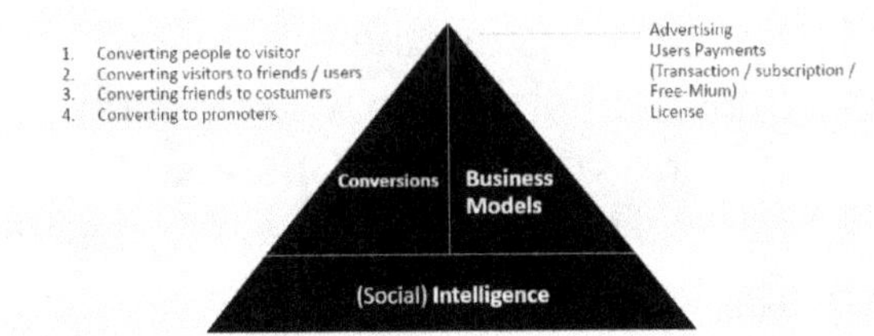

Any digital enterprise, business or brand that decides to implement a digital strategy to improve its business should address the following three main components:

1. **Gathering information**

   Every company should step into Big Data by acquiring intelligence and in-depth acquaintance with consumers and potential ones. Social networks have significantly improved our ability to meet our target audience and know them for the purpose of developing a relationship or a marketing dialog. Without this ability and its assimilation into the company's ongoing activities, no successful business can happen in the digital age.

2. **It's all about conversions**
   Creating a relationship between brand / business and consumers is an essential condition for any marketing activity. This

relationship should be based on the brand's continuous and evolving presence on various digital arenas where it meets its customers (as opposed to the old approach of campaign snacks).

Consequently, the brand or company should produce four work plans:

Converting people to visitors – the first work plan will outline the activities that will ensure people will get familiar with the business digital arenas and recognize the value they get from the brand. This work plan includes programmatic advertising, organic promotion, sponsored promotion, social marketing, mobile marketing, Influencers marketing, electronic public relations and the like.

Converting visitors to friends, followers or users. The second work plan will focus on ways to turn your visitors into friends or users. In other words, the beginning of a dialog and the initial basis for a possible relationship. This plan will concentrate on content and initiatives to provide visitors with value, allowing them to return and bring along their friends. The better we get to know these visitors, the more likely we will be able to provide them with targeted content and value which will do the job.

Converting friends or followers to customers. The third plan on this side of the triangle attempts to get brand followers or users to become customers that generate direct or indirect revenues for the brand. How is this done? Usually with simple moving/business-oriented trigger tools which move users from a place devoid of any brand business model to a business-selling dialog venue. For example: coupons that move the user from the brand's Facebook page to the brand's digital store or to a retail chain where the products can be bought.

Converting customers to brand promoters. The fourth plan is based on the assumption that marketing success in the digital age cannot be completed without a move to convince enough users, friends or customers to support the brand and become its promoters. To achieve this, you, the passionate customers should be located (perhaps the most important segment of the digital world). This is the most significant move in order to create an effective marketing plan for the return on marketing investment. If you can get enough people to be your brand promoters, your marketing success is guaranteed.

How is this done? Provide your promoters with value and attractive content, reward them and develop long-term relationships with them.

They will do the work for you.

3. The third side of this triangle points at the need of every digital initiative for a **business model**. In other words, a clear understanding of the potential source of the company's revenues. It can be an advertising-based business or one which relies on direct user payments (subscriber fees, purchases or a freemium model that combines free use with paid upgrades).

These models currently control most digital businesses that appeal to consumers. Other models can also be found, such as license-based revenue from the use of technology or content. One way or another, a digital business should establish a valid business model, preferably with more than one revenue source.

Our recommendation – draw your business triangle with the details relevant to your business. Make sure you cover all of the elements listed. Are you doing it effectively and sufficiently? What are you missing in order to build a stable and healthy digital business?

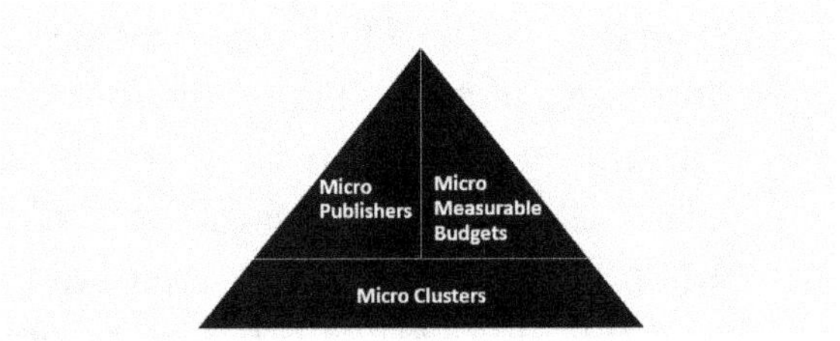

The second triangle refines the most important and unique characteristics of the digital market.

Mass Marketing is dead & the end of spray and pray

These insights have led the industry to consider a different path. No more trying to hunt down as many people as possible and yelling at them telling them how good we are.

The digital age demands (and, of course, allows) the selection of a specific and accurate **micro-segment** as a target audience, to recognize it, value it, gain its attention and develop a relationship that will enable a successful marketing-business dialog.

This is the ultimate **EMF** in the age of digital – **Effective Marketing Flow: Familiarity-Value-Attention-Relations-Marketing dialog.**

For example, designating **women** as a target audience does not apply anymore. Not even **pregnant women** as such. An effective digital plan requires us to pinpoint a more specific and accurate audience, for example: **women pregnant with their first child**. This is a micro-segment or a micro-cluster with highly defined characteristics, with very similar needs, anxieties, desires and cravings. This is a micro-segment format which allows you to come up with a set of added values and customized content to gain their attention and create a genuine relationship.

After choosing a micro-segment (or a number of micro-segments, usually for multi-brand companies), we select the communication channels with which we are looking to create a dialog with our target audience. You cannot reach a micro-segment through large media companies. This is done through the new type of media – the **micro-publishers** – Influencers, bloggers and content and community creators, who might not appeal to the masses, yet gain attention and response, sometimes admiration, from the audience we are eager to reach.

The first side of this triangle deals with the precise definition of the target audience. The second side focuses on the correct media strategy for the digital age.

Based on the triangle's first two sides, the structure and nature of the media budget is set. Avoid putting your money with a company which provides the results of the marketing activity after the deed is done. The current approach is all about micro-budget (i.e. we pay a blogger $5,000 per post), measured and managed, based on quantitative and qualitative goals.

To summarize the marketing triangle – micro-clustering which you achieve through micro-publishers following a micro-budget plan of activity.

Our recommendation:

Examine yourself – have you defined at least one micro-cluster you intend to look at and develop a lasting relationship with? Do you know how to reach that audience through dedicated, precise communication channels while paying them considerable attention? Is this move based on a sensible budget plan?

The Social tringle
Brand's Social Marketing evaluation & planning

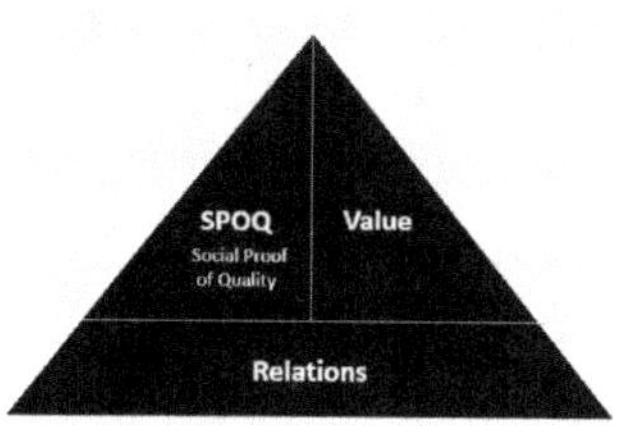

This triangle examines your social networking activity and how well you utilize the behavioral profile of potential customers, in an era when people value brands based on their perceived value, user feedback, and comments.

The first side of this triangle reflects the perception that what people say about a product or brand affects buying decisions much more than any advertising campaign of a company and brand. People who use the product or service are the most reliable witnesses about its quality. This is the reason the marketing arena is beginning to focus more and more on the term **Social Proof of Quality – SPOQ**.

SPOQ is a super-term that describes all the channels through which people influence others in their purchasing decisions and preference of a product or service. Brands and companies realize that they have to be involved in this process and to address users' responses posted on the web as a resource or threat. No one can ever ignore the power people have over our buying intentions and realization. The experience of customers, users or buyers is the most significant configuration of the significant domain Of UGC – User-Generated Content.

The second and third sides of the triangle present the assumption that no marketing can happen without creating a relationship with its target audience. That means that brands should generate intrinsic value for its customers or potential ones. In the digital world, intrinsic value is usually expressed in the creation of content or content tools relevant to the brand.

Our recommendation: Check your SPOQ Index score. Are people talking about you? What is the sentiment involved? Are you in control of this important factor? Do you have a plan to encourage and distribute good feedback? Do you provide your customers with value beyond your product?

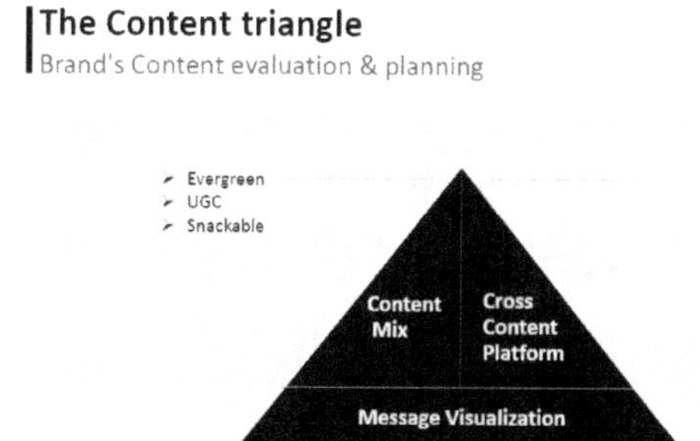

More and more companies are beginning to act as publishers. The content strategy of companies, businesses and brands in every sector is based on the following triangle:

The **content mix** should include "**evergreen"** – such that can be used as ammunition over time. Another item that has to be part of your content work plan is, of course, User-Generated Content (UGC). This is the most popular content among users, which they are more likely to share and distribute.

Another relevant point worth mentioning is that content strategy, is what we call Snackable content – short, targeted and wrapped in a user-friendly package.

The second leg of this triangle emphasizes the fact that brands should invest in visualization of their communication with their target audience with video being the most popular and sharable type. The good news is that producing video and images has become easy and cheap.

Another requirement resulting from the way media is consumed today is the need to be present on **all platforms** relevant to your target audience. A cross-platform strategy is needed whether you are a big or a small company.

Our recommendation:
Make sure you have entered the content area structurally and seriously. Are you consistent in creating content for your customers? Do you have an accurate content strategy including an effective

content mix? Do you know how to distribute it?

E Commerce Triangle
Digital shops evaluation & planning

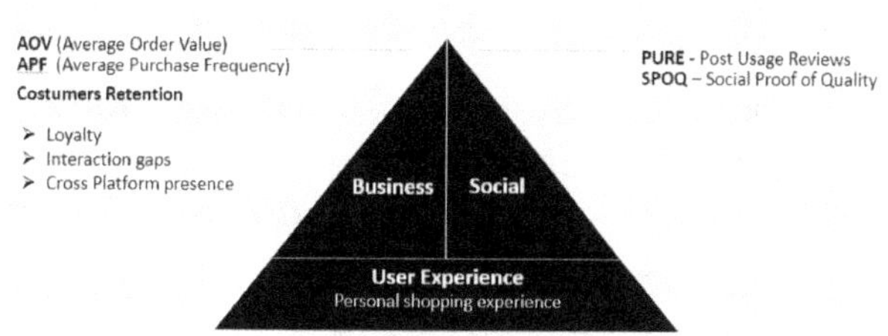

The success of a digital store depends on three pillars that you should consider for your store:

1. From a business point of view, you need to measure and improve APF – Average Purchase Frequency as well as the AOV – Average Order Value. From a business-marketing standpoint, it is very important to retain existing customers with activities such as frequency of contact between interactions, a loyalty club, and of course, cross-platform presence in order to increase the chance of meeting customers on any platform they are on.
2. In terms of social feedback volume, a digital store should work to improve factors such as:

Post-Usage Reviews & Social Proof of Quality. One follows the amount and sentiments of users' feedback, while the other is the quality index compared to your competitors.

3. **User Experience** – It is possibly the primary advantage of the digital world. Accessible technologies enable digital storeowners to offer their customers a personalized store – with a tailored design, unique shelf layout and, of course, relevant sale offers based on an in-depth familiarity with their characteristics, needs and expectations.

Summary

The marketing and media industry is going through its most interesting time ever. We are at a tipping point after which the relationship between brands and media companies and consumers will change completely.
The one-track marketing communication gives way to a relationship based on deep acquaintance, value and continuous dialog. The digital natives set the tone in key areas such as media consumption, content creation, digital shopping, social interaction, and cultural and consumer trends.

Brands, advertising agencies, and media companies need to internalize these changes and adopt new practices and methodologies if they wish to stay in the game.

This book addresses a variety of these new insights and methodologies outlining the best practices and trends for marketers and media professionals who are looking to prepare themselves for the new age.

One-trick ponies – those who are focused on one unique skill, talent, ability, quality – cannot deliver the goods anymore.

Marketing and media professionals should be committed to a diverse specialization that covers all relevant areas: advertising with its various types, content-based marketing, Influencer marketing, mobile marketing, social marketing, and e-commerce specialization.

The book provides the new marketers and media professionals with tools for understanding and assimilating the five main legs of the field.

About the author

Ofer Oved

Lives in Israel. Works in Europe & USA.

An experienced C-Level executive – AOL, McCann Ericson, HIRO Media, Noga Communications and other large companies and start-up companies.

A lecturer– Digital Media & Marketing and Innovation.

A mentor and consultant for start-up companies in Israel and Europe.

A Writer and Editor of an Israeli Media, Marketing and Innovation blog (Romi Media).

An expert in the fields of Digital Marketing, Social Media business, Mobile Marketing, Digital Content and TV.

Email:

contact@romi-media.com

About Westech Media

Westech Media is a digital marketing agency in the UK that specialises in promoting small and local businesses.

Over the last ten years it has helped hundreds of clients to grow their businesses, increase their sales and gain more customers.

If you are a small business owner and would like assistance promoting your business then contact Westech Media today.

www.ingramcontent.com/pod-product-compliance
Lightning Source LLC
LaVergne TN
LVHW020041110826
845155LV00029B/580